The
Ever Speaking
Voice of
God

BY

NITA JOHNSON

THE EVER SPEAKING
VOICE OF GOD

Nita Johnson

ISBN# 0-9656528-2-3

Edited By: Madeleine Thomas, and Ricci Wilson

Cover Design & Desktop Publishing By:
Gary Grubbs, Freestyle Graphics
1334 S. 119th St. • Suite B• Omaha, NE 68144

World for Jesus Ministries, Inc.
Eagles Nest Publishing
643 North 98th Street • Suite #146
Omaha, Nebraska 68114 – U.S.A.
Office (402) 498-3496
Fax (402) 331-5375
E-mail: nitawfjm@aol.com

New Address Effective as of September 1998.
MSC #402
497 - N. Clovis Ave. #202
Clovis, CA 93611-0373

THE EVER SPEAKING VOICE OF GOD

DREAMS, VISIONS AND VISITATIONS FROM THE LORD

INTRODUCTION

The book of Joel lists various types of communications that the Lord would open to the Church in these last days. Verse 28 of chapter two reads as follows:

And afterwards I will pour out My Spirit upon all flesh; and your sons and daughters shall prophesy. Your old men shall dream dreams, your young men shall see visions. V29. Even upon the men-servants and maidservants in those days will I pour out My Spirit. V30. And I will show signs and wonders in the heavens and on the earth, blood, and fire, and columns of smoke.

The word "vision" in Hebrew is *hazon*, which means vision—a sight mentally, i.e. a dream, revelation or oracle. The Greek word rendered "vision" is *optasia*, which means visuality, apparition. Thus, a vision is a divine revelation containing a visual message from God.

The word "revelation" comes from the Greek word *apokalupsis*, which means to uncover, unveil, or to disclose. It conveys the idea of a revelation being a *communication of the knowledge, wisdom, insight of God to the soul.* When speaking of a vision, this revelation is being said to have been communicated to the sense of sight. Further, we learn in Revelation 19:10b *For the substance (essence) of the truth revealed by Jesus is the spirit of prophecy [the vital breath, the inspiration of all inspired preaching and interpretation of the divine will and purpose, including both mine and yours].* So, when Jesus is speaking in such a manner so as to reveal His divine purpose or plan to the senses of man in such as a vision, we can be confident that it will line up with the over-all counsel of God and will edify or instruct us in truth.

The Lord has chosen to speak to me in all these various ways primarily for the instruction and edification of the Church. I cannot say that God has given me this grace for any peculiar righteousness of my own, as I am still vulnerable to failure just as you are. The Lord has simply granted this grace in mercy for His Church.

This book therefore, is a compilation of dreams, visions and visitations that have been divinely granted to me for you. I will only include those that Jesus specifically gave for the body of Christ for edification, instruction, or discipline. I will omit open visions, or what I call visitations that I received for my own personal edification, or what I may have received for a certain individual regarding a specific situation, as they are of a private nature. Further, I will not as a rule, include many visitations that I have covered in other books.

I will include Scripture references that will further clarify or confirm a certain insight if I feel that it may be beneficial to the reader. Further, if I feel it may be helpful for me to share my understanding of a certain experience, I will do that for the advantage of the reader.

I trust you will find the information both interesting and informative. My purpose in compiling this book is to allow all those who have an ear to hear, to hear the insight that may pave the way for growth in your Christian life. Further, some of the information I received from the Lord demands a quick alteration of the hearer's direction and lifestyle, and is therefore critical information for many in the body of Christ to receive. Finally, I have composed it by the Lord's direction, with the promise that He would supply what would be needed to put it in your hand. He further promised that He would send it forth on the wings of eagles just as He did my book "Prepare For the Winds of Change." I trust that in reading the following insight, you will quickly make any adjustments the Lord may require of you for your well-being. By obeying the Holy Spirit's prompting and making any necessary changes, you will keep yourself in the way of safety and life during the troubled times which lay just ahead of us.

I give you this book which in some respects reflects my deeply personal and intimate relationship with my dear Savior, in the greatest love for your own pilgrim's journey. I pray that you will receive it with the love with which I endeavor to give it to you. May God bless you in your reading and in your seeking as you attempt to implement the values of these revelations into your own life.

Your Friend,

Nita Johnson

Nita Johnson

5

1958 A VISITATION

"BLESSED ARE THEY WHO DO NOT SEE"

When I was but eight years old, I was out in my front yard playing when I looked up into the sky, and hovering right above me was Jesus. I cried out: "Jesus, you are real! There is a real Jesus!" He smiled and said to me: "*Nita, behold the nail prints in My hands, and look at My side where they pierced Me with a sword.*" I cried: "my Lord and my God." He replied to me: "*You see therefore you believe, blessed are they who do not see yet they believe.*" (John 20:27-29) Then He left!

A few minutes later, He appeared again saying: "*Nita, look at the nail prints in My hands and see here the wound in My side where they pierced Me with the sword; and be not faithless but believing.*" I cried out again: "Jesus, You really are real. There really is a Jesus. My Lord and My God." To that He repeated: *You have seen, therefore you believe. Blessed are they who do not see yet believe.*" He then left.

I share this with you, because so many in the Body do not receive visits in this way from our Lord. For that reason they feel they are not as valuable to the Lord as those *who do see Him.* The truth is just the opposite. Blessed are you who do not see Him, yet believe Him and take Him at His Word. There is a special blessing upon those who fit into this category. It is a blessing that you will see in heaven. Our faith is to the Lord a most important commodity. He cherishes it as much as He does our very soul. So, I want to invite you to read, be instructed and enjoy the entries in this book. Let them spur you on into a deeper seeking of the Lord for yourself.

Jesus once told me that He was going to use me as a testimony of His grace. Through me He would make His Church jealous in order to spur her into a deeper seeking of His face. Then He would be able to begin to reveal Himself to others in His Church, as He now does to me. In the end however, whether you see Him or you don't, you are much loved by Him in a most tender way. Use the things you read to minister to your heart of His great and incomparable love.

—— ✦ ——

12/79 VISION

"PERSECUTION"

I had been in a time of fasting and prayer about the future of our country. The Lord decided at that time to give me the first of many revelations about our tumultuous future. I saw soldiers from China as they were moving across America. I saw some of them go up a hill to a Christian's home, force the man out of his home and try to make him deny his faith in Christ. When he wouldn't do it, they beat him to death before my eyes. So, I was taught that America will be under siege by China. During the course of that siege, there will be Christians who will give their lives for Christ. (Matt. 24)

Just prior to that time, the Lord is going to clean up the leadership of His Church through a great revealing of unrighteousness. I saw leaders who were impure and some who were in reality serving Satan. The Lord would do this to protect the innocent sheep. Those who are really desiring Jesus and not to follow after man, will run from these impure leaders and be brought in under the protection of true shepherds just in time for a very treacherous time for the Church. (Zech. 11:8)

---- ✦ ----

2/80 A VISITATION

"GO, HEAL THE SICK"

I was asked by a friend to go and pray for two different people. One was an elderly man, the other was a little baby. Both were hours from death and both families had been prepared for this eventuality. I had never prayed for the sick before, so, I didn't know what to do. But I had heard that an English man by the name of Smith Wiggelesworth would always ask the Lord if He wanted to heal the person he was invited to minister to before he would go and pray for them. Then according to the Lord's answer he would know whether he was to pray for them or not. So, feeling very frustrated at being asked to pray for two people so close to death when I had never before prayed for anyone, I sat down on my family room sofa and prayed. As I prayed I wept through my frustration, hence Jesus appeared to me. When I saw Him, I told Him what I was going through, and wanted to know what to do. He looked at me with great kindness in His eyes. He said: *"Nita, any time someone asks you to pray for them, you are to go. Don't be concerned about whether or not I want to heal them. Just simply go in faith that they will be healed, I'll take care of the rest."* As His words entered into my heart, I knew that this was a commission for His body. We are all to do the same, go and let Jesus take care of the rest.

Incidentally, I did go to pray for both of them. The results were: the elderly man went home to be with the Lord, even after experiencing a tremendous healing that resulted in one doctor becoming a believer. The little baby went home to be with her parents in just a day or so, well on her way to being totally healed. (Matt. 10:8)

——— ✦ ———

2/80 A VISION

"WARNING FOR AMERICA"

I was sitting alone in my family room in prayer when suddenly the Lord opened up to me His decree for America in a profound vision. First, everything in the temporal world disappeared and I saw only black. My mind went blank, if you will. Then, in a split second of time, I saw out in front of me the United States seal, rolling end over end. As it moved closer to me it seemingly increased in size until it stood the size of a man. It came to a standstill about two feet from me, then disappeared.

Next, I saw a black leather Bible. As it came nearer, it looked like someone was thumbing through the corner of pages in rapid succession. It too increased in size until it was the size of a man. Coming to a standstill about two feet in front of me, it then disappeared.

Then, the Cross appeared. It too came from a great distance away. Just like the previous two visions, the Cross began a great distance away and began to slowly move closer to me. It came to a standstill, again about two feet in front of me. Simultaneously, a voice that sounded as though it was echoing down through the ages of time, spoke the words: *"Liberty through Christ Jesus.*" I saw the same words appear in an arch over the Cross. Then the Holy Spirit spoke to me, giving me.:

In the freedom Christ has made us free [and completely liberated us]; stand fast then, and do not be hampered and held ensnared and submit again to a yoke of slavery [which you have once put off].(Galatians 5:1.)

———— ✦ ————

4/80 A VISION
"THE WORD IS SPIRIT"

I was sitting in church at the time and listening to the minister as he was exhorting from the Word. I noticed a cloud of light coming from his mouth, so I asked the Lord what He was showing me. Then I saw the word S-P-I-R-I-T flowing out of his mouth in the cloud. Then I understood that the ministry of the Word is spirit and we should when it is pure doctrine, embrace it with all our hearts that we might grow and be nurtured thereby.

It is the Spirit that gives life [He is the life-giver]; the flesh conveys no benefit whatever [there is no profit in it]. The words (truths) that I have been speaking to you are spirit and life.(John 6:63)

———— ✦ ————

6/80 A VISION
"GOD'S TRANSFORMING LOVE"

I had been intently praying that the Lord would give me a greater understanding of His transforming love. When I least expected it the

Lord gave me a vision to help me understand the answer to my question.

Suddenly a friend was standing before me in a very clear open vision. She was a person who was very troubled. I don't know what happened to her in her childhood years, but whatever it was it left her a very troubled adult. Yet, she was likable. Let me try to explain. She was a person who tended to see the negative side of things. She was also an alcoholic. She often complained about anything and everything, yet she had a great sense of humor. I suppose that was the main reason people liked her. She had a pretty face, but she was terribly over weight and stooped shouldered. Although, she was not always unhappy, her entire countenance was one of a general overall pout. So, here she was in front of me, in all of her pain, holding in her hand a can of beer. As I sat looking at her, the Lord told me to love her. I said: "I can't Lord. I can have pity for her, but I can't love her."

The Lord began to give me a series of exchanges through which I would soon see my friend transformed before my eyes. I was told to replace the beer in her hand with a glass of water, self-hate with a godly self-love, and fear with trust. Peace and a sense of well being were to replace her deeply rooted anger and bitterness. Next the Lord told me to fill her with joy and a sense of expectancy about her future and watch the depression leave.

Suddenly my friend was surrounded by a group of people who really loved her. I could see her loneliness evaporate as she reached out. Love seemed to emanate from her to the people in her world. She changed before my very eyes. She stood two inches taller, and lost about fifty pounds. She was utterly irresistible. Again the Lord said: *"Now love her!"* Immediately, I became filled with love for her, and cried: "I do love her Lord, I feel as though I am going to burst!" Then He replied: *"that is how I love you! You have seen the power of My transforming love. My love flows down over your soul revealing sin and injury. As you let Me heal the injury and remove the stain of sin from which you have repented, you are wonderfully transformed into a vessel of love unto My honor!"*

———— ✦ ————

"KINGS CROWN"

I saw a vision of a king's golden crown. It was very ornate and quite beautiful. Next, I saw a golden scepter such as a king would use. Again, it was ornately decorated, yet it spoke of authority and power. Finally, I saw golden vessels such as would be in a king's house. Then a voice quoted (I Kings 10:21):

All of King Solomon's drinking vessels were of gold, and all the vessels of the House of the Forest of Lebanon were of pure gold; none were of silver: it was not accounted of in the days of Solomon. (I Kings 10:21) K.J.

The fact the vessels, king's crown and scepter were ornate was indicative of the great trials that these vessels would go through in preparation for their forthcoming. There will in fact be vessels of silver, brass, wood, hay and stubble. But, none of these will rule from the King's house, as the golden vessels will. The difference in the authority and power of the golden vessels compared to the silver vessels will be as day and night. Finally, as I understand it, it is indicative of the great Apostolic Age.

—— ✦ ——

"THROUGH THE EYES OF LOVE"

I was wrapped in an experience of the Holy Spirit; perhaps we could call it a trance. (Acts 10:10) I both saw a vision and experienced a great touch of My Savior that left me inquiring into things I was not hearing from the pulpit.

I stood up in my Sunday school class, which had about 350 people. I was shy and because I was so young in the Lord, I felt very insecure about sharing my experience. Nevertheless, I stood and began to share. "Last night the Lord let me see the way He sees us." I began: "Through the eyes of love and through the blood of Christ, the Father sees us as righteous. But, because He is God and can see and does know all things, He also sees all of our sin. He knows every bit of sin we will ever commit for the rest of our lives. So, He sees us both holy and sinful at the same time. This is the difference between positional righteousness and conditional righteousness. Again, it's the difference between being righteous by faith in Christ's blood and being experientially holy. So, He sees the positional righteousness in which we stand because of the blood of Jesus. But God also sees the condition of our unrighteous hearts. This is where His love comes in. Because of God's great love for us, He chooses to see us through the blood, until He can perfectly cleanse us of the unrighteousness that is in our hearts. Further, it is by His love that He heals us of our sinfulness." With that, a torrent of the Lord's love swept through me so powerfully, that my spirit left my body and began to ascend toward heaven. But, I grew fearful and thought I was dying and going to heaven for good. I didn't want to do that because I wanted to finish raising my daughter. So, the Lord let me come back to my body.

Notwithstanding, I was left with a real need to understand how the Lord's love cleanses us. And, I wanted to understand through the Scriptures, the difference between righteousness and holiness. These were subjects which I continued to pray over until the Lord began to teach me through His Word, through additional experiences and through giving me intellectual understanding.

—— ✦ ——

5/81 A VISION AND A VISITATION

"THE LIFE OF CHRIST"

In the season of my rebellion, I lived a very worldly life. Once I came to the Lord I quickly moved into a life of practical holiness. My worldly ways began to drop off very quickly, as I had such an intense love for the Lord, all I wanted to do was to please Him. The greater my love and dependence upon Him grew, the more I struggled over my old life. It was so painful to think I would ever do anything to hurt Him, that I couldn't forgive myself for the many ways I had hurt Him in the past. For this reason, I would spend much time telling Him how sorry I was for my past life of sin and selfishness.

The time came that my Savior desired for me to finally be set free from this awful bondage, so He in His great kindness decided to speak to me about it.

I was in prayer one morning, when I began to see out in front of me like watching a movie; The Life of Christ.

I saw only brief pictures of His earlier years. As a child He was wise far beyond His years, and a child of unbelievable love. He not only desired peace, but he was able to make peace wherever He went. He was able to settle disputes with a few well-chosen words and bring peace where once there was disputing. He did not have a lot of friends that He regularly associated with however, but was more a loner, as He enjoyed just being in the presence of the Father. He simply did not seem to enjoy a lot of things that other children loved to do, and that limited His playmates. He was always very kind to all. For that reason when other children wanted to take sides against one another, they knew they could not expect Jesus to join with them. He would not take sides but instead, provoke to peace. Again, that would force Him to at times stand alone. Jesus seemed to have difficulty understanding a great deal of our egocentric ways even as a young child. But, His kind and winsome ways won Him favor with older children and adults alike.

I saw His love for the Father from His earliest days. He loved to hear the Law being spoken and He loved to go off on His own and spend time with the Father. The Bible tells us of a time when Jesus was twelve years of age; Joseph and Mary found Him with the elders and teachers of the Law in the court of the Temple. The questions and answers that He spoke were so filled with the wisdom of God that the men marveled at His understanding. His understanding came out of a heart that was filled with the love and wisdom of God. He knew Him as He spent much time with Him being trained by the Holy Spirit in the ways of God. He had nothing in His heart to marr love, no covetousness, pride or earthly passions. He was as pure as the Bible states.

The love I saw in Him both for God and for man was so extraordinary. He never preferred Himself. He never had a care about earthly things. He never desired to own anything. All of His care was set upon the Father and doing His will, and upon people. He was a man of uncommon kindness, courtesy, and gentleness. Even in reproof, the compassion and love that was evident in His tone and clearly seen in His eyes, made you want to accept even the most difficult things to hear.

I saw Him as He walked with His disciples. The love and care that He always demonstrated for them was again, extraordinary. He taught them continually, not only with His words, but also in all that He did as He walked before them. It was little wonder that they wanted to be near Him. I would see them say silly things, such as the Bible records. For instance, I saw them disputing over who was the greatest among them. Then I saw Jesus demonstrate with a little child, the beauty of humility in the Father's eyes. But, He did it with such kindness and gentleness, that it was disarming. His love for them was unrelenting and tender. I was allowed to see Him as He was attacked by the religious leaders of His day. It was difficult to watch, but amazing to see His heart as He responded to them. Though His heart was filled with love for them He would at times respond in rather cryptic tones. Even when He was angry at the religious bigotry in which they were so entrenched, He cared deeply for the sake and condition of their souls. It was out of this deep care for them and righteous anger at the lies that kept them bound that He would speak to them with such severity. He was attempting to cut through the hardness of their hearts and religious pride. Alas, only the resurrection ultimately freed some of them from their self-righteous delusion. One might think that after some of the frontal attacks that Jesus endured at the hands of His persecutors that He might have a great deal of difficulty working through forgiveness. I was amazed to see that this was not the case. Because of our Lord's deep humility and gentle meekness, He never stumbled over bitterness. Jesus' love for the souls of His persecutors never wavered and His mercy toward them ultimately seemed to be the very balm that would heal the pain of their tongue-lashing and the satanic darts, which were flung at His heart through their verbal abuse. I sat in awe as I watched this drama unfold.

I saw His amazing love for the woman caught in adultery. While her accusers stood around her with hearts filled with pride, self-righteousness and hatred for this poor lost sheep, Jesus loved her. I saw the commandment that He wrote in the sand. I realized that it was not the words that Jesus wrote that caused her accusers to turn and leave, but the conviction of the Holy Spirit that came upon their hearts exposing their individual sins and revealing that they were indeed as guilty as she. That moment was a wonderful victory for the mercy of God. This woman was so grateful for our Lord's love that she repented and was changed.

Jesus was a continual story of the miracle of divine love. Everywhere He went and all that Jesus said and did, was divine love personified in humble human form. My heart was exploding with such love for my Savior I hardly felt that I could contain it. Tears of gratitude for His simple, pure and unselfish love were flowing down my face.

I continued to watch as the evening of the Last Supper drew near. I saw how Jesus drew aside a great deal more with His disciples. His life with them became more private than public as Jesus sought to prepare them for the task that would follow the resurrection. Our Lord's care and concern for His disciples was so evident. He loved them without reserve right up until the end. Not until His struggle in the garden did Jesus display any care for Himself at all. Every minute and every hour was spent in caring for those around Him.

I watched them as they partook of the Last Supper. Then I saw as Jesus spent a great deal of time talking with His disciples in preparation for the approaching hours of pain and uncertainty through which they would travel, knowing all that would befall them in those great hours of darkness. How tenderly He loved and cared for them. Although Jesus knew that they would all in essence forsake Him in His greatest hour of need, His love for them was unwavering. Jesus demonstrated not an ounce of bitterness, anger, aggravation or resentment for the failures in which He knew they would all participate before the crucible would come to an end. He was as tender toward Judas, knowing that he would betray Him, as He was toward all the others. Jesus never showed any concern for Himself until the struggle in the garden. Even then His greatest concern was that He would do the will of the Father.

The scenes of the mock trial, the beatings and whipping that Jesus endured passed before me in rapid succession. Before I could even contest, He was hanging on the Cross before me. I looked at His poor mutilated body; His brow ripped by the crown of thorns the men had gouged into His head. I saw His beautiful face once so filled with joy and love, now so filled with pain. The swelling, bruising and disfigurement of His gentle face was so horrible to look upon. My heart was literally breaking as I looked upon Him. The pain I saw in His badly swollen and bleeding eyes was excruciating. I was weeping uncontrollably. I wanted it to come to an end. I was allowed to feel a very small degree of the pain Jesus experienced as our sin was cast upon Him. Oh, the anguish! I could only compare it to pouring acid into an open wound, so horrific was the pain. I saw as the satanic kingdom hurled their torments against my Savior! It was like great ocean waves of liquid fire with the sounds of anguished voices screaming in the night that flooded over Him repeatedly. Voices, but no faces. It was all satanic torments. (Ps. 22:12-16; 88:7,8,14-18) Jesus' soul quailed under it. But, never did His love waver for mankind who had nailed Him on the tree. Finally, I heard Him say: *"Father forgive them, for they know not what they do."*

I was by now so gripped with anguish over His suffering; I was beside myself. Suddenly the Father's voice broke through my churning emotions saying: *"Spit on Him!"* "What!" I thought. Then He repeated Himself to me. I cried: "No! I won't. Look at Him ~ His anguish, His poor mutilated body. No, I won't." The Father again demanded of me: *"Spit on Him!"* I cried out: "How can You ask me to do that? Lord, I love Him, and look at His suffering." This I replied as I looked back at my tortured Savior, tears streaming down my face, my heart filled with such pain at my Savior's suffering. Again, the Father spoke to me:*"Nita, spit on Him!"* "No", I replied in deep sobs of grief: "I love Him I won't add to His suffering, I won't." The Father then tenderly spoke to me: *"That is what you are doing when you won't forgive yourself. Nita, that is why My Son endured all this pain, that you might be forgiven for your sins. For His sake, I have forgiven you and delight to do it. Now forgive yourself and be free of your guilt! "*

Oh, the amazing love of the Father, the Son and the Holy Spirit. Never would our God desire that we labor under guilt for sins for which we have been forgiven for Jesus' sake. Finally, I was set free of the guilt and pain of the wasted years. I was free to love and be loved by my wonderful Savior. I hope this will help you as well. I would like to add here, that the forgiveness for which Jesus died was not only for the Father's forgiveness of our sins, and our forgiveness of ourselves, but also our forgiveness of others. It is so very important that we don't wound the One who was wounded for us by refusing to forgive those who have transgressed against us.

---- ✦ ----

5/81 A VISION

"THE SPIRIT OF SODOMY"

I was in prayer over America when suddenly I saw out in front of me a map of the United States. The map was sectioned off into states, but that was not the important message. What I clearly saw hovering over the map was the message that God was seeking to give. Stretching from end to end, its head on the West Coast, its tail on the East Coast, was a dragon. It looked like the dragon that often appears on Chinese paraphernalia during the Chinese New Years parade. I asked the Lord who or what it might be and what it meant that it was extended from coast to coast. His answer was immediate: "it is the *'spirit of sodomy,'* and *it rules America from coast to coast. It is the reigning prince over America. Its name is 'Rothshawn,' which means, "Head of the Goats."*

———— ✦ ————

8/81 A VISITATION

"GIVE YOURSELF"

I was getting ready to move out of my home. I was told to sell it and give all to the poor as part of the preparation process I was to go through to prepare for full time ministry. I had done fairly well in the Real Estate Business, so I had a pretty nice home. At the time I was still very young in the Lord and was very dependent upon material things as a means of security. Further, although I did not realize it at the time, I needed a lot of healing which I have since undergone, to correct some faulty thinking, so I felt quite fearful about my future. One of the things I was so terribly concerned about was the fact that I knew that in moving from my home, I was closing the door completely to my old life in the business world. I would no longer be financially comfortable and free to spend money on whatever I might want or want to give another as an expression of my love. I would be moving into a life of personal poverty.

As I was packing and preparing to leave my much loved home, I was gripped with fear. The main fear with which I found myself grappling with was how I would be able to show people that I loved them since now I would have no money to freely buy them gifts. I became so overwhelmed with this fear, that I crumbled to the floor weeping profusely. I cried out to the Lord: "Lord, now that I am poor, how am I going to be able to let people know that I love them. I will have no money with which to purchase them gifts?" I felt so utterly desperate and quite alone. My Master was kind enough to come to me and help me through my dilemma. I saw Him walking down the muddy streets of Jerusalem with His twelve disciples. His feet were muddy, as was the hem of His garment. I saw the multitudes pressing against Jesus demanding of Him. Each one seemingly so needy. He would walk and talk to His disciples, stopping when needed to minister to people. He would heal the sick and comfort those who were needy. He was constantly giving of

Himself to all that He met, if not to strangers, He was giving to His disciples. Suddenly He stopped what He was doing and looked straight at me. Then He so tenderly spoke: *"Nita, give yourself."*

I stopped weeping and pondered what He said. Jesus then smiled and left. His words seemed to alleviate my concerns for the moment. Although it felt a little strange as I realized that I didn't at that time feel that I had much to offer. Further, I feared that anything I might want to give of myself would probably not be enough in the eyes of other people. Yet, if that was all I had to give, I could only hope that it would in time be enough. So, I was starting a new day and walking a new way.

Although this particular visitation was on a more personal level, I felt that it would minister to many who are yet to understand that they too are valuable to the body of Christ. Not because of remarkable gifts or talents, and not because they might have a lot of funds that can be given to help the work of the Lord. But, because they can give themselves, and in doing so have given the greatest gift of all.

---- ✦ ----

9/81 A VISITATION

"HIS HOLINESS"

We had temporarily moved in with my sister. I was spending many hours in prayer and in the Word each day in preparation for answering the call that was on my life. I had repeatedly sought the Lord to help me understand the difference between holiness and righteousness. I was still an infant in the faith and had heard no one ever speak on the subject of His holiness. In the 70s and 80s all people were saying was that we were the righteousness of God through Christ, and that was all we needed. The implication was that we did not need to worry about the sin in our life, and we were to quit being sin conscious. Don't worry about cleaning it up; just forget that it is there because God no longer sees it, as He sees us through the blood of Christ. I couldn't accept that as I saw too many times that the Scripture spoke both of holiness and righteousness, at times referring to the need for both in the same Scripture. In addition, I had experienced some things with the Lord that told me I greatly needed this understanding. So, I prayed and continued to pray that God would give me understanding of the difference between the two and His requirement of us in this area.

The house was now empty as everyone had gone away for the evening, my daughter included. So, I went out to my sister's living room and began to walk around just worshipping Jesus. Eventually I moved into worshipful adoration of Him. I was singing a song about His holiness. As my Lord's holiness began to enter into the room increaseing in its manifested presence, I could no longer utter the word, holy. The very word began to be too holy to be spoken from the defiled lips of a human being. I had never felt this presence before, so I didn't necessarily know how to respond to it. But, I knew I couldn't speak of this holiness with my mouth. So, I continued to worship Him, but no longer with my mouth, only my spirit. I walked and worshiped while the manifested presence of my Lord's holiness continued to increase. As this continued, I began to shake. I was experiencing a fear of Him.

Suddenly, Jesus came into the room. He was wrapped in a cloud, as it were, of His holiness. Before I could even think about what I was doing, I fell to the ground, and lay upon my face with my hands extended. I trembled violently for the fear of His holy presence. I was terrified! I lay before Him unable to speak for fear that if I did, I would die. My sinfulness became extremely apparent. It wasn't as though I could tell you every secret sin that was in my heart. Rather, I felt my utter sinfulness as a human being. Further, I could see it in light of His utter, moral perfection, the majesty of His holiness. He was so holy, I feared dying every moment I was in His presence, because of my sinfulness. Consequently, I laid there trembling saying nothing for fear I would die if I did. I wanted so badly to speak to my Savior, for I loved Him. To be in His presence and unable to tell Him how much I loved Him was unbearable.

As I lay there, I knew that I was before the One Who held the universe together, as I could feel such a power emanating from Him. I knew He held the universe together in His belly. I understood that He held all created things together with His Word because He was holy. Nothing and no one could successfully contest His majesty and right to rule, for He was the beginning of all things, and His holiness was so perfect, no created thing could ever hope to touch His supremacy.

Finally, my need to communicate with the God whom I loved and sought to serve with my whole heart was so overwhelming; I found the courage to speak to Him. Again, not from my mouth as He was too holy, for me to do that, but from my spirit I said to Jesus: "Lord, I love You, I want to talk to You but, I am afraid that if I do, I will die. I want You to talk to me, but I am afraid if You do I will die. I want You to stay, for I love You so much but, oh how I want You to go, for I fear if You don't I will die."

He began to speak to me from His Spirit to mine and revealed some things to me. Then He said: *"Nita, I am going to return to My Church with this presence, but, not now."* I asked Him why He was going to wait. He answered: *"Because, if I returned now, many of My people would die for the sin that is in their life."* He then gave me a message out of Deuteronomy chapter five for a church I was going to be ministering in the following Sunday. Then He left. I just lay there shaking for a very long time. It was many hours before I quit shaking. Every time I even thought about Him, I would start shaking all over again. I couldn't speak about anything holy for many days without trembling.

The next morning before dawn, while I was sound asleep, the Lord came to me again in the same presence. This time He wrapped me in a cloud of His holiness. I was elevated off my bed and enswathed in His holiness. Again, I began to tremble violently.

He spoke but a few words to me then left. From within this cloud came a voice that sounded like it was reverberating down through eternity, saying: **"My Word Is Holy!"**

I could not talk about what had happened for many weeks. The first time I even tried: I spoke to an elder of our Church who had been in the faith for some forty years. I wanted to know what had happened to me. As I tried to share my experience, I began once again to tremble so violently, that it took a very long time to finally share what little I could. He stood in amazement as He listened to me. Finally, he told me that God had come to teach me the fear of the Lord. His words of comfort aligned with what the Lord had spoken to me (*Fear not, God has come to prove you so that the [reverential] fear of Him may be before you, that you may not sin.*).

—— ✦ ——

7/81 VISION

"A VISION OF HELL"

I had been praying for the lost when suddenly I was thrust by the Holy Spirit into travail. The spiritual veil was then removed and I found myself standing at the mouth of hell, and looking straight into the lake of fire. I saw men, women and children of every race on earth. They were screaming in terrible anguish. I'll never forget the sound of their awful cries or the look of anguish on their faces. Matthew 25:41b *Be gone from Me, you cursed into the eternal fire prepared for the devil and his angles.*

---- ✦ ----

10/81 VISION

"WORSHIPPING ANGELS"

I joined a circle of people who were singing. As we sang, the Holy Spirit pulled me to the center of the circle to lead the group in worship. The next thing I knew, I was in heaven directly above our circle of worshippers and had become a part of a group of worshippers there. As we continued to exalt the Lord together in song, a group of angels encircled us, joining in our worship to our great King. Before long, another even larger group of angels joined and also began to worship our Lord. Each group sang in a different heavenly language, however we all blended so beautifully. It was the most exquisite harmony of worship I have ever heard. Then I saw Jesus our great Lord and Master come near. His appearance inspired a whole new dimension of worship from us and we entered into heights of worship that are beyond human expression.

When I returned to the saints on earth the Lord told me, that when His children humble themselves to worship Him on earth from a pure heart, it engenders worship from saints and angels alike in heaven. They virtually gather together above the earthly pilgrims, joining in with them to adore our Savior!

---- ✦ ----

2/82 A VISITATION

"JESUS COMING SOON"

I was in prayer over a series of meetings that I was conducting, seeking the Lord over what He wanted me to say to the people of this fellowship. One morning He appeared to me. He was standing in a threshold such as would hold a door. I asked Him: "When is the time of Your coming?" He answered me by saying: *"Tell My people that I am standing at the threshold and I am coming soon."* With that He stepped over the threshold with His right foot, then disappeared.

I am coming quickly; hold fast what you have, so that no one may rob you and deprive you of your crown. (Revelation 3:11)

——— ✦ ———

FALL OF 82 A VISITATION

"A VISITATION OF GLORY"

I spent many hours in prayer every day, as I loved being with Jesus more than I desired to eat. At this time however I was in prayer for the Church I was ministering in. I was staying in a motor home in the parking lot. Toward the end of my prayer time, the Holy Spirit came in like a mighty rushing wind, and shook the motor home like a bomb had exploded inside of it. I felt the wind seep through my feet, and I fell on my face before God. Then my entire being was on fire with the glory of God. I could physically feel the fire upon my members. I was under such an anointing that I could hardly stay conscious and was unable to stand without aid through the entire service.

I was ministering on the Holy Spirit. Some 42 people received the Baptism of the Holy Spirit that night. Further, many miraculous healings occurred. After the service, as my friend and I were walking back to the motor home, two men came who were drunk and tried to run us down. Three times they tried, but we were able to get away and back to the pastor's home on the other side of the Church so the police could be called. I suspect that Satan didn't like the great victory we had experienced that night.

7/82 VISION

"A VISION FOR REVIVAL"

My precious Lord called me to intercession for America. As always, the minute He called, I dropped the thing I was doing and went to meet Him. I spent nearly five hours in prayer. Of those five hours, I spent nearly two hours in deep travail for America. During the final one and one half hours I invited two friends to join me as the travail was simply too heavy for one person to bear on their own.

Just as the travail was about to come to an end, I was given a vision. I saw the heavens aflame with the glory of the Lord. It was breathtaking to behold. Suddenly, the heavens rolled back, leaving an opening that looked like a fire had burned a hole through a veil. The Holy Spirit then descended in the form of a dove. As it reached earth, this dove released a glorious outpouring of revival upon man.

7/82 A VISION

"REVIVAL AND JUDGMENT"

I saw revival sweep over Japan, France, and the United Kingdom in a wonderful display of God's love. Then I saw a wonderful outpouring in Russia. This was accompanied with much persecution. In spite of this persecution, I saw that the saints were as bold as a lion. They continued putting out the net of life regardless of the cost, bringing many into the kingdom. As a result, there was a great harvest of souls. I saw many miracles in these countries, for God was with the saints in great power.

Then I saw judgment begin to fall upon America. As this cycle progressed, I then saw a great outpouring of revival with great miracles accompanying it begin to flow over America. This brought The Church into a time of great harvest. After the revival had progressed for a bit persecution broke out against the Church in America. Through the combination of the greater manifested presence of our Lord and the persecution that we were being afflicted with, I saw the Church enter into a deeper level of holiness and by far greater and more sublime purity.

—— ✦ ——

7/82

"THE MEEKNESS OF CHRIST VS. HITLER'S LOVE FOR POWER"

I was meditating upon Matt 11:28 through 30. I was longing to understand the humility and meekness of my dear Savior. Slowly, His meekness began to enter the room wherein I was in prayer. As this occurred, I found that I could no longer sit upon the sofa I was sitting on, as I felt too elevated before His meekness. Consequently, I moved down to the floor. A few minutes passed, and I began to get too uncomfortable sitting on the floor. Even here I was above His meekness. So, I lay prone, face down on the floor. After another few minutes, I felt very uncomfortable and had a real need to hide myself under the carpet, so I began to weep as I had no where to hide. I spoke softly to Him telling Him how I felt too lifted up. I told Him that I wanted to be as meek as my Savior is, but I felt that I couldn't possibly get beneath the meekness of My Lord. I told Him that it felt like if I were to climb under the floor, if that were possible, that I still could not get beneath the meekness of the Lord. My heart overflowed with love for Him, and my appreciation of His character was greatly enlarged. I began to feel wrapped in His peace, a peace that flowed out of His meekness. I lay continuing to meditate upon His meekness allowing myself to as much as possible be absorbed by it. I was becoming meek, desiring to serve, to give, to suffer whatever may need to be in order to help and heal the unfortunate plight of another. I was loosing a sense of self-consciousness and self-preservation. I wanted only the good for another.

As I was becoming totally absorbed by this presence in my inner-man, without warning everything began to change. The atmosphere, rather than being one of the peace and gentleness of the Lord was becoming violent, filled with anger, pride and dictatorial control. Just as the nature of my Savior's meekness had begun to be a part of me, now this other nature was becoming a part of me. I wanted power at any cost. I began to feel so hungry for power that I could have murdered to have it. What I wanted, that was all that mattered. How I loved power and hated people. The more I grew in love for this power, the more I grew in disdain for people. People were simply a means by which to get whatever I may want. Anything to exalt me, is what I lusted for. What I needed is what mattered, regardless of what another might have to suffer to provide it. I was insane with a love of power, ravished as it were with the very thought of increasing my rule and my kingdom, until I could rule all.

When this experience had reached a peak, and I really could no longer handle what was occurring inside of me, the Lord spoke audibly to me. He said: *"Nita, what you are experiencing is a love of power to its extremity. This lust will even murder to satisfy its ravage hunger. The one absorbed by its folly is unreachable, as they are so filled with pride they think they are invincible and cannot be wrong. That was the heart of Hitler.*

"On the other hand, you experienced My meekness. This holds within its bosom a love for people that will compel the bearer to give his own life if need be, to provide for the honest needs of another. Seek My meekness and never allow a love for power to enter your heart."

—— ◆ ——

8/82

"A HEAVENLY VISIT"

I was in worship prior to a time of ministry in a Church in California. As I was adoring my Lord, I suddenly found myself lifted up in the spirit and transported to heaven. Initially, I could not tell where I was standing. However, I could see the streets which were made of transparent gold. Behind me was a huge edifice, which appeared to be some sort of meeting place in which the saints would perhaps gather to worship the Lord as an assembly. It was glorious to see and had a look of grandeur. Beside me were huge apparently white marble pillars. These pillars were so large I could not have put my arms even half way around them. I saw people walking in and out of this place, talking together as they walked along. Everyone seemed busy and happy.

Other buildings that I could see were beautiful. Everything had sort of a translucent glow about it. The peace that was there was remarkable. I could feel it and see it on the faces of all that passed by. This peace and sense of well being was so profound that I felt as though Jesus Himself were all around me. In fact, although I did not see Him face to face, I felt as though I had just spent time with Jesus, as everything seemed to speak of Him. Further, I felt such a love and divine protection for this place and these people. I knew that I was feeling the heart of my Savior for His own. The Holy Spirit then spoke to me so clearly that it seemed as though He was right in front of me. He said: *"This is Zion."* Immediately after, I found myself back in the Church filled with the joy and presence of my Lord."

— ✦ —

8/82 A VISITATION

"JESUS SUFFERS FOR THE LOST"

I was in prayer for an individual whom I knew to have a tremendous call upon their life. They were struggling, wanting to attend Bible School in the Midwest, yet, not wanting to give up the things of the world by which they were unfortunately bound. In the midst of my praying and weeping over my friend's quandary, Jesus appeared to me.

He was weeping, and His middle was missing. It was as though someone had taken a hole right out of the middle of my Savior. As I looked at Him, I was confused, but it broke my heart to see Him weep. I asked Him: "Jesus, why are you weeping?" But, He wept still! By this time the pain of seeing my Lord weeping was more than I could bear. So, I was in deep tears of agony seeing my Lord and love of my heart in such pain. I pleaded with Him: "Jesus, please tell me why you are weeping."

Finally, He replied: *"Tell (D) that I cannot be filled without the precious souls for which I long, and for whom I died. I will never be complete except they fill Me with their presence in the kingdom of our Father. To see them eternally lost, is a pain that is more than I can bear. I weep that (D) might answer the call I have placed upon his life: and I weep for those who are lost and in darkness waiting to be led into the light for the salvation of their souls."* (Ezekiel Chapter Three)

You might ask, why if this word was for another, do I share it with you? I do so, because any time a person does not answer the call that God has placed upon his life, and for which they were created, precious souls remain lost to the kingdom that were to have received light through that person had they been obedient to the call. Today, if you know that God is calling you to follow Him in the ministry, please yield your life to Him and trust Him to help you be faithful to His vision.

—— ✦ ——

9/82 A VISION

"THE ARMY OF GOD"

I was standing at the pulpit singing with the congregation a song about the army of God, when suddenly I saw a vision. As the scene opened, it was dusk and was swiftly being overcome by the darkness of night. I saw the army of God coming up over the hill. This army was fully clothed in the armor of God and shined with splendor and radiance from the glory of the Lord that covered each member. This glory was not just something that was coming from the exterior however, but was coming from deep within their persons. By the time the army had fully approached the top of the hill, it was dark all around. But because of the light that shined from this great military force, it looked as though the sun was dawning over the horizon in early morn. The sound of their footsteps echoed with such thunder, that the army dressed in black at the bottom of the hill turned, and gasped with a look of horror at the approach of their converging enemy. It was a beautiful sight to see.

They run like mighty men; they climb the wall like men of war. They march each one [straight ahead] on his ways, and they do not break their ranks. v8) Neither does one thrust another, they walk every one in his path, and they burst through and upon the weapons, yet they are not wounded and do not change their course. v9)They leap upon the city, they run upon the wall, they climb up on and into the houses, they enter in at the windows like a thief. v10) The earth quakes before them, the heavens tremble. The sun and the moon are darkened and the stars withdraw their shining. v11) And the Lord utters His voice before His army, for His host is very great, for [the enemy is] strong and powerful who executes [God's] Word.(Joel 2:7-11)

———— ✦ ————

3/83

"A CRITICAL WORD OF WARNING"

I had been invited to meet with an individual who was the coordinator of many of the top ministries in America. The purpose of this visit was to possibly let him take over coordinating my own ministry. I was praying about this, as it would mean a major thrust out into front line ministry and major visibility in the body of Christ. Consequently, I determined that I would not accept this invitation unless the Lord Himself said to go.

Having spent hours in prayer about this subject, the Lord finally spoke. When He did, it was the Father who spoke, and He spoke audibly. In the voice that sounded like many waters He said: "Ministries made of man will fall in this hour!" Well, that took care of that question. I suddenly realized, upon receiving this word that if we were to allow this person to take over our ministry, that is what we would have when it was all over; a ministry made of man. I trembled from the sound of the Lord's voice. If you are just now starting out in ministry let the Lord build your house, so you don't end up building it in vain.

Except the Lord builds the house, they labor in vain who build it; except the Lord keeps the city, the watchman wakes but in vain.(Ps 127:1)

SPRING OF 83

"THE APPROACHING KING"

I was ministering in a Church in Oregon at this time. The whole congregation was in worship and the presence of the Lord was so sweet. I felt compelled to open my eyes as previously I had been worshipping Jesus with my eyes closed and was fully lost in adoring my Savior.

As I opened my eyes, it seemed as though I had been transported to another place of worshippers although I knew I had not. The saints in our Church were all worshipping Jesus with hands lifted to Him in one way or another in adoration. But, as I opened my eyes I saw the saints with large palm branches in their hands waving them up and down slowly as though they were worshipping an approaching king. As I watched, I soon saw my Lord Jesus walk into the building and come down the aisle, walking between the outstretched palm branches. He was dressed in royal King's garb and was exuding a magnificent love for His people as He enjoyed their worship. He was there it seemed, to answer their entreaties. Then I understood. The Holy Spirit spoke to me saying: true worship escorts the King into your presence. (Ps 22:3)

———— ✦ ————

6/83 VISION

"VISION OF REVIVAL"

I saw awesome miracles taking place by the prayers of men, women and children alike. People who were lame and maimed from different kinds of things that had left them disfigured such as accidents and so on, as well as people who were maimed from birth defects were all miraculously healed. I saw miracles with inanimate objects for the sake of winning a couple of Satanists to the Lord. I saw signs and wonders with nature. I saw huge football stadiums full to overflowing with people, signs and wonders of every sort were happening. Miracle healings such as the healing of advanced stages of leprosy, cancers of every sort, AIDS, strange diseases that were extremely rare but killers of mankind, and other miracles which pertained to the human body. Creative miracles such as limbs suddenly being placed where no limb had been before. Faith was high and so was the power of God. Miracles were taking place in such dynamics that the secular press wouldn't stay away. They wanted to film and broadcast it internationally. The media had become a friend to the Church for a season. Everywhere you would turn, you would see awesome miracles taking place. Through the prayers of children, young people and adults God was being glorified in these miracles. I saw men, women and children walking up and down rolling hills with their arms lifted high worshipping their Savior in wonderful and beautiful worship that sounded so sweet, it sounded like the angels were singing.

Love abounded through the Church as hospitals were being emptied and peoples' lives were being put back together. I saw the press virtually running here and there to get the latest story on the creative miracles that were taking place. I saw Churches reaching out in missions in an unprecedented way. Finances were pouring into the Churches everywhere and the money was going back out to missions at home and abroad. Prayer was going on night and day. Television was taboo, and in its place people were praying, wrestling with the powers of darkness for souls. Oh it was wonderful! Jesus was being proclaimed everywhere. I saw people being bodily transported for the sake of winning souls to the Lord. Further, when people were transported or met with people who couldn't understand their own language, the Lord was giving the gift of tongues so that the Gospel could be preached in the language and dialect of the hearer. It was a most wonderful display of grace the Church had ever known. And the most wonderful display of Christ the world had ever seen.

The Vision came to an end!

— ✦ —

8/83 AN OPEN VISION

"THE LIFE OF PETER"

The vision started with the earliest days of Peter's relationship with our Lord. Peter was first introduced to Jesus by his brother Andrew.

(John 1:40-42) Peter almost immediately received the Master's call by which he was forever separated from the secular life to share our Lord's burden to preach the good news of the Gospel of peace to the whole world.

Peter loved Jesus more than any one he had ever had occasion to come to know in the past. He loved him with a true zeal that not even Peter understood. Peter frequently found himself in situations wherein he would verbally burst out with whatever was on his mind quite sure it was the right thing, as his words usually came out of inner explosions of love, which he was feeling for Jesus.

It was this very nature that Jesus loved about Peter. He was an all or nothing kind of guy and the Lord knew that when this nature was properly harnessed by the Holy Spirit, Peter would run the race, as few others would do. Indeed, Jesus saw Peter as a diamond in the rough. Although he was at the time, pretty rough, Jesus could also see what Peter would become before he would go home to be with our Lord. So, Jesus brought him into the inner circle of leadership. Indeed, Peter would be the very spearhead of moving the Gospel forward after our Lord's ascension. Jesus planned it that way. All of Peter's little mistakes would be inconsequential in the light of the overall picture.

I saw as they walked and talked together. Jesus would frequently when speaking with Peter look into his inner-most heart. This would totally unnerve Peter. But, then Jesus would smile at him calming Peter's fears. I watched as Jesus taught Peter, at times pulling him aside alone or with James and John. At times like these, Jesus would speak with much greater intensity. His teaching would be of greater import so as to incite Peter's faith. When Jesus would see Peter step out in faith above the others, Jesus would always secretly rejoice. He was not rejoicing because the others did not, but a joy that Peter took the plunge. At times such as when Peter was walking on the water and failed, Jesus would reprove him, but secretly He was smiling that Peter dared to believe at all. Every lesson on faith was very important. Sometimes, Peter would seem as dull to the reality of what Jesus was trying to teach him as could be. So, again Jesus would reprove him. However, when by our Lord's reproof, Peter was stirred to a deeper probing of spiritual things until he could understand, Jesus would be exceedingly pleased. Seeing that pleasure in his Master's eyes, would mean more to Peter than Peter knew how to tell Him.

Peter had an ambition. That ambition was to be pleasing to Jesus. Many of his lopsided remarks and tendency to overstep his bounds came out of that zealous desire to do and say whatever might please the Lord.

They had a truly unique relationship. A relationship that was shared with none other. I was often given the ability to feel what was going on in our Lord's heart toward Peter. At other times I would be allowed to feel what Peter was feeling during their interaction. The love that Jesus had for Peter was joyful and expectant, at other times kind and gentle, but, always full and overflowing.

The love that Peter felt for Jesus could be described as explosive, intense consuming, and so he was literally consumed. He was a man of passion, and he had a passion for Jesus.

It seemed Peter traveled through a million emotions. He wanted always to do what was right, and what was expected of him. When Jesus would teach on faith, Peter wanted to move mountains with his faith. When Jesus would teach on forgiveness, Peter would tear himself up, until he could find his way through to forgiving someone with whom he may have felt hurt. He never wanted to say no to his divine Friend. He loved being with Jesus. In fact, he wanted to spend every waking moment with Him, learning about Jesus, the Father, and the things of the kingdom, even though he didn't necessarily understand all that Jesus attempted to convey. When he would be alone at night, he would contemplate all that had occurred and everything that was said during the day trying to glean as much understanding of these things as he could. There seemed to be no words to express how he loved our Lord. He had mountains worth of love, but was a little immature in wisdom.

The time was to come that Jesus would begin to speak to His disciples about His soon coming crises. Sometimes when Jesus would mention it, it seemed to go right over Peter's head. Other times when our Lord would begin to share about this difficult time, a dart of pain would go through Peter's heart. Sometimes, Peter would do nothing more than grimace, other times he would find himself unable to contain and he would speak out. It was at a time like this that he was so severely reproved by our Lord. Peter's human compassion wanted to spare Jesus the suffering. This I found has been a fault of most of us. We very much want to protect our loved ones from pain and suffering. Further, he unwillingly tried to quiet the pain that had just lanced his own heart at the thought of losing his friend. Peter didn't understand the divine plan that he was in through his relationship with Jesus any more than the other disciples did. Jesus indeed reproved Peter, but He did it for Peter's sake as well as the other disciples. Learning to accept suffering as part of the Christian experience was vitally important for all of them. Although Peter received the Lord's rebuke it didn't at that time give him much more understanding of things. In fact the whole episode brought some painful confusion to Peter that would not be cleared up for a while yet.

From that point on, Peter wrestled with the near future, not really understanding the pending turn of events and concerned about his possible loss. Questions began to arise in his mind about the Kingdom and what it must mean. Would he rule with Jesus? Had their understanding about the Kingship of Jesus been correct, or what was Jesus talking about when He referred to the kingdom?

At this point many questions began to arise. These questions and concerns however, would not be answerable until after the ascension.

As time rolled on and Jesus set his face toward Jerusalem and the cross, His time was dedicated more toward instructing His disciples than ministering to the crowds of needy people. For that reason, the disciples were able to ask more questions. Through this personal attention, as well as the Father determining that it would be a time of further opening their understanding to things, more of their confusion began to be cleared up. Still Peter wondered at the thought of how Jesus being their Messiah could possibly be determined to die.

The night of the last Passover finally came, and they were to share a very special meal with Jesus. It was one to which they were all looking forward. As the meal progressed and Jesus began to share regarding His coming crucible, Peter was startled. How could this be? He really was going to lose Jesus? Then Jesus speaks of Peter's own failure: *Simon, Simon (Peter), listen! Satan has asked excessively that [all of] you be given up to him [out of the power and keeping of God], that he might sift [all of] you like grain, But I have prayed especially for you [Peter], that your [own] faith may not fail; and when you yourself have turned again, strengthen and establish your brethren.*" (Lk. 22:31 & 32) Peter, stunned at the news that Jesus had just reported was quick to remind our Lord of His own commitment to die with Him if necessary. And Simon Peter said to Him, Lord I am ready to go with You both to prison and to death. Jesus wouldn't let it rest. He pressed, not to make Peter feel or look bad. But, Jesus desired to let Peter know that His love and care for him, as well as the call that the Father had placed upon Peter's life was not depended upon Peter's love and faithfulness alone. But it was dependent upon the Lord's will and keeping power which He effected by His own grace. Further, he would in the end come to see that our Lord's love for him was not based upon Peter's perfect behavior, but on the Lord's own eternal character and the preciousness that He saw in Peter in spite of his failures. But Jesus said, "*I tell you, Peter, before a [single] cock shall crow this day, you will three times [utterly] deny that you know Me.*" (Lk 22:34) A knife as it were, went through Peter's heart. How could Jesus say that he would forsake Him? Did Jesus really not understand how much Peter loved Him? After all this time when Peter had stuck by Him through thick and thin, did Jesus really not understand that Peter would give his very life for Him. Peter felt so hurt, yet he pondered the fact that Jesus had never yet been wrong about anything. Still he would do all he could to prove Jesus wrong this time. Peter would not leave Him when Jesus needed him the most. This is why the Bible records that Peter was so near our Lord as the terrible events that prefaced the actual crucifixion occurred. Peter was near when all others but John had abandoned Jesus because with all of his heart he didn't want to forsake the Lover of his soul.

The Lord had set the clock and the hands were turning. Nothing it would seem, would stop the awful clicking of those eternal hands until all that was intended was complete. The dinner now being over, Jesus gathered around Himself a towel and instructed His disciples to prepare for what He was about to do. One at a time Jesus knelt and quietly washed His disciples' feet. As he approached Peter however, Peter bade Jesus to stop. "Lord are my feet to be washed by You? After Jesus reproved him, Peter went a little further saying: you shall never wash my feet. In the Greek a better rendering might be something to the effect of; by no means to the age. I consider it below your dignity. Jesus' response was immediate: You do not understand now what I am doing, but you will understand later. Peter felt a need to let his divine Friend know how much he loved Him and thought of Him as was fitting. So, Peter said to Him: *"You shall never wash my feet!"* Again our Lord quickly replied: *"Unless I wash you, you have no part with (in) Me [you have no share in companionship with Me]."* Simon Peter said to Him: *"Lord, [wash] not only my feet, but my hands and my head too!"* Finally Jesus calmed our bewildered Peter down with: *"Anyone, who has bathed needs only to wash his feet, but is clean all over. And you my disciples are clean, but not all of you."* (John chapter 13)

After assuring His disciples of His eternal care, He let them hear His foreknowledge of events about to take place, that they might know when all was finished that He was in fact the promised Messiah. Jesus began to feel deeply disturbed in spirit, at which time He told His anxious disciples: *"I assure you, one of you will deliver Me up [one of you will be false to Me and betray Me]!"*

After Judas left the table and went out into the night to betray our Lord, Jesus once again reiterated His love for them and gave them further instruction to love one another, as He had loved them. Peter at once took this opportunity to remind Jesus of his own love, saying; I will lay down my life for You. Jesus then knowing that His disciples were all anxious and very confused, comforted them, further instructed them, and then prayed over them as recorded in John chapter 17.

From there Jesus took Peter, James and John with Him and went deep into the garden to pray as His own heart was breaking for pain. He instructed our sorrowful Peter to pray that he might not enter into temptation. There, Jesus was filled with such sorrow as He wrestled against the powers of darkness that were seeking to dissuade Him from the cross. Jesus fell into such agony of mind as He wrestled that the Bible says: He began to show grief and distress of mind and was deeply depressed. Then He said to them: *"My soul is very sad and deeply grieved, so that I am almost dying of sorrow. Stay here and keep awake and keep watch with Me."* Drawing aside a short distance away, Jesus fought the battle of the ages that He might stay true to the commission of His Father. So great was His struggle and agony, that He began to sweat great drops of blood as His body moved into full distress. In His tender mercy, the Father sent an angel from heaven to strengthen our Savior.

Where was Peter? He was asleep with James and John. Not for lack of care and interest however, nor was he just being lazy. It was *grief* to which he was reacting. Seemingly all too soon the prayer and preparation time was at an end, for Judas and those sent by the chief priest were at hand. So, Jesus awakened His sleeping friends one last time and led them down to meet the approaching crowd.

As the situation began to get heated, Peter moved valiantly into dealing with the whole situation in the flesh, and drawing his sword cut off the servant's ear. It seemed that everything he had been taught for the last three years was of no value. In his distress he rose up to take control of a situation he could otherwise do nothing about. But, Jesus remaining calm as a result of the praying in which He had just engaged, healed the servant's ear, and calmed Peter down.

As Jesus was led away to the High Priest where He would be beaten, Peter and John followed. They wanted to stay near in case they could be of any help. But, as destiny would have it, it would be here in the courtyard of the High Priest's home that Peter would be tempted and fall. Seeing the gravity of danger that Jesus was in, Peter became frightened. Turning from the zeal to protect his divine Friend, he moved into self-protection. Jesus was suffering at the hand of His accusers. His face was bearing the marks of their abuse. Peter could hear just enough of what was going on to push him into deeper fear. One by one people began to ask him if he was part of Jesus' company. Just as Jesus told him he would do, he denied that he even knew Jesus three times. After his third denial I saw him turn to look at Jesus. Jesus' eyes met Peter's. Then Peter remembered what Jesus had told him he would do. Further, Peter realized that Jesus saw him deny Him. As their eyes met a dart of shattering pain went into Peter's heart. He let Jesus down when Jesus needed him the most. His heart couldn't take it. He broke with grief, and ran away to cry out his pain alone.

You can't possibly imagine what Peter was feeling at that moment. The depth of his pain was beyond my ability to bear. I not only saw all this, but I felt the pain that ripped through Peter's heart when he realized what he had done and to make matters worse, Jesus had to see him do it. His love for Jesus was so deep and all consuming, that he couldn't bear having failed Him. I wept as I saw this drama unfold and felt what Peter was going through. I wept for Jesus, and I wept for Peter. What a dilemma to be imprisoned by, to have to chose between your life and the life of your dearest friend; a friend that had become dearer to you than a brother. When you thought you had the strength to choose Him, and you find out that instead you choose yourself and let Him die alone at the hand of His persecutors. The grief of guilt, and the heartbreak of feeling like a traitor to love is overwhelming. You can only walk through it to understand what Peter experienced.

I saw the look in our Lord's eyes as He looked at Peter. His eyes were filled, not with the pain of just watching your friend betray you, but compassion. I saw so much compassion for Peter. Then I was allowed to experience what was going through our Lord's heart. Compassion, His heart was so filled with love and compassion for Peter. Jesus knew how much Peter loved Him. He understood how badly Peter wanted to be there for Him. He also knew how Peter would crucify himself a thousand times over for his failure. All that insight filled Jesus' heart with compassion for his bereaved friend. Jesus hurt as much for Peter as Peter was hurting for what he had done.

I saw Peter run into the darkness, crumble against a wall and wail with such grief, my heart couldn't take it. I was weeping so hard I could barely see the vision that was before me. Peter's deep and incessant grief continued, the anguish of his failure consumed his entire being. How many times he cried out: "if only it could have been me instead of You Jesus." The time came when they were to hang Jesus upon the cross. His body was beaten and battered. His face swollen, bruised, lacerated and bleeding. His own anguish already beyond description. As they hung Him upon the cross, I wanted to die inside from the anguish I saw rip across His poor swollen face. Peter also saw it and crumbled and wept bitterly for his divine Friend. As our Lord's body became disjointed from the impact of the cross falling into the ground, it was too much for me to handle. I couldn't watch. I wept and wept. As I regained the courage to look back to the drama that continued to unfold before me, I saw Peter, head in hands weeping, his body convulsing under inner-anguish. He would look up at Jesus, then put his head in his hands and cry. Finally, our Lord's Spirit left His body, and His body was at peace. But, Peter would not know that peace for a long time to come.

Finally Jesus arose! I watched as the angel revealed himself to Mary, telling her to go and tell the disciples and Peter that the Lord had risen and that Jesus would go before them into Galilee. I watch as Mary went back to relay the message to the disciples and Peter and John bolted out of the door to head to the tomb. When Peter arrived to see the stone rolled away and the tomb empty, I saw wonder and amazement in his eyes.

After several appearances of our Lord to His disciples, He later found them at the lake fishing. This was to be a very important day for Peter, for it was the day that Jesus would finally heal him of the critical guilt and grief that riddled Peter's heart. After the fish were cooked and eaten, I saw Jesus and Peter sitting off and kind of alone together. The discussion in which they would engage would be designed to reestablish Peter in the ministry and to bring healing. This is what I saw occur.

Jesus said to Simon Peter: *"Simon, son of John, do you agape (love) Me more than these others do?"* Peter replied: *"Yea Lord you know that I phileo (the love of a friend) You."* Jesus said: *"Feed My lambs."*

Again He said to him a second time: *"Simon, son of John, do you agape Me?"* Peter replied: *"Yea, Lord, You know that I phileo You."* Jesus said: *"shepherd My sheep."*

He said to him a third time: *"Simon, son of John, do you phileo Me?"* The Bible says that Peter was hurt that Jesus asked him the third time if he had *phileo* for Him. But, this is what I saw. Peter began to cry. All the grief that had been stored up over the past days came flushing to the surface. Jesus had pointedly and purposefully pegged Peter where he was. Now they both knew that Peter's love was of a sort that would never be able to live up to Peter's own expectations. His love was not any greater than the others. His love was weak and would break down again and again under such heavy pressure as it was subject to during the Lord's crucible. Jesus always knew this, now Peter knew it and together they shared this understanding. Peter no longer had anything he needed to prove to Jesus. Jesus accepted him right where he was. And Jesus said to him: *"Feed My sheep."* Then Jesus gave Peter hope. He told him that the day would come when he indeed would give his life for his Master. Therein would the (Agape) love that Peter longed to give our Lord be complete and be given full expression. The day would come that divine or agape love would fill Peter's wings and carry him to places others would never go. At last the agony was over, and Peter was healed and accepted by his Lord, just as he was.

Then the day of Pentecost had fully come. The disciples received the power from on high and were released to fulfill their calls to make disciples of all nations for Jesus. Peter who had been the one who was tried the greatest would be given the greatest anointing. So much so, that people would be healed by his shadow.

Some time later, John and Peter were walking up to the gate Beautiful, where laid a man who had been crippled from his birth. Peter looking at him, said to him: *"Silver and gold I do not have; but what I have, that I give to you: In the name of Jesus Christ of Nazareth walk."* What the Bible doesn't tell us, and what I saw taking place in Peter's mind was this. As he said, Silver and gold have I none, but what I have I give unto thee rise up and walk, Peter saw what was indelibly inscribed in his mind until the day he gave his life for Jesus as a martyr. He saw His Lord hanging on that cross, His face bruised, lacerated and swollen, with blood streaming down His brow. He saw the mutilated body of Jesus convulsing under the agony of the inhuman tortures He was being subjected too. He saw the tears streaming down our Savior's face as Jesus cried out *"Father forgive them."* He saw and understood how his dearest Friend had undergone all of this so that the soul, the spirit and the body of man could be healed. With tears of gratefulness and a heart full of the Lord's own compassion, he told the man to, in the name of his most loyal and divine Friend, rise up and walk, being made free of the horrible bondage of his years of suffering. The scene of our Lord's crucifixion never left Peter's mind. In fact it was at the forefront of his mind the rest of his life. It was for the reason of his own failure and the love that he knew he never deserved, that Peter when himself crucified, would not allow them to hang him on a cross in the same fashion in which Jesus gave His life. Instead, he insisted on being turned upside down and hung on the cross to die in that manner, to make his life a sacrifice of love for his Lord and Master.

Peter failed, but Jesus used that failure to lift Peter into a wonderful and powerful ministry to thousands upon thousands of people for the rest of his life.

—— ✦ ——

"THE INTERCESSOR"

While ministering at a Bible School, the Lord awakened me in the middle of the night to a remarkable vision of the Old Testament High Priest fully adorned in his priestly garb. While the vision was beautiful in itself for the beauty of the High Priest garment, it was extraordinary as this High Priest radiated with the glory of Heaven.

As He stood before me, the Lord began to illuminate the Scripture to me explaining what each piece of the garment represented to the New Testament Priest.

He began with Ex. 28:1. The Bible states that the garment was an adornment of beauty and glory. This represented the fact that when an intercessor enters his prayer closet to intercede for another, standing in the presence of God, he is adorned in glory, God's own glory which He has conferred upon us. This glory Jesus paid the price of His own blood to provide. It is beautiful in the Lord's eyes. Further, it is a garment of light. This makes it powerful to the detriment of our enemies who cannot overpower the light.

The colors of the garment are gold, blue, scarlet, purple and white. The colors reflect the following: gold, is for His deity, the Author of our authority. Blue, is for His throne which is in heaven, and the position of our rule. Purple signifies His royalty, the headship of our rule. Scarlet represents the blood of Christ, which gives us the right to rule. White reflects Christ's imputed righteousness, our covering and eternal destiny to rule.

The "Ephod", which was a beautiful jacket that was worn over the linen robe, was gold, blue, scarlet, purple and fine twined linen, which was white. The breastplate of judgement, which carried upon it the Urim and Thummim and the twelve stones of Israel was worn upon this jacket. It speaks of God's zeal for His own. (Is. 59:17) Further, it speaks of the High Priestly or Mediatorial work of Christ. This is the work the intercessor is engaged in during their time of intercession on behalf of another. We are mediating the mercies of God toward that needy soul. The coat of many colors, which caused Joseph so much trouble with his brothers, was likened to it. This type of garb was always given to the son who would be carrying on the priestly ministry of the family. This was a position that was normally reserved for the eldest son and for that reason ignited the jealousy of the other brothers. So hear we see that the intercessor is clothed with this same priestly garment in the picture of the "Ephod".

The next item He expounded on was the *"Breastplate of Judgment"*. Among other things, it does have one outstanding benefit, that of carrying the judgment that belongs to another upon the intercessor. You might say, how could that be? When we go in before the Lord to pray for the mercy of God upon someone who has transgressed against us in some way and having forgiven them we are seeking the Lord's forgiveness and blessings upon them, we have in essence carried their judgment upon ourselves. This is what Abigail did before David when her husband sinned against him. When we pray that God will forgive the sins of our forefathers entering into perfect identification with them, we are in essence carrying their judgment upon ourselves. It is only because of the blood of Christ that we are able to do this. Because we are covered with His blood we can enter into the throne room to seek God's forgiveness for another. You might say, that on the one hand we enter wearing the *Breastplate of Judgement*, on the other hand, the *Breastplate of Righteousness*. For if we are not covered with His blood, and do not bear this breastplate of mercy we can be no intercessor before God.

Further, on the *breastplate of judgment*, we find the twelve stones that represented the twelve tribes of Israel. But, for us these stones represent the twelve virtues of Christ. These are peace, joy, suffering-love, humility, righteousness, goodness, grace, mercy, justice, compassion, truth and forgiveness. As we wear these before the Father, we are standing in the perfection of Christ. We are not here to speak evil of our brother, but to intercede for our brother in love. Also upon the breastplate were the *onyx stones*, which were wrapped in pouches of spun gold. These stones carried upon them the names of the twelve tribes of Israel, and were worn into the holy of holies as a memorial unto the Lord. The spun gold represents the heart of the intercessor. It is to be a heart of pure love for those for whom they intercede. The stones speak of the Cross of Jesus Christ. As an intercessor we carry the cross of another person's burden upon our shoulders. It is frequently a cross, requiring self-denial in order to pray through the burden of the one for whom we intercede. It is very pleasing to the Lord. (Mt. 16:24) Further, the *onyx stones* bear the names of the 12 son's of Israel. These names upon our *onyx stones* are representative of the perfect government of God. When we intercede for another, we are not to intercede for our own plans in his life; but we are to plead for the will of God, that they may be reconciled to God's perfect will or government.

Also on the breastplate hung the *Urim and Thummim* these stood for the spirit of truth, or the Holy Spirit and truth. It was through the instrumentality of the *Urim and Thummim*, that the Lord would speak to the High Priest giving His direction concerning issues at question. Now we have the Holy Spirit and the Word; and the Bible says they will always agree. By these means the Lord will speak to the heart of His own making known His will. This is especially so when in intercession for a specific thing that requires an immediate answer.

The *"Linen Robe"* is symbolic of the righteousness of God that is imputed to us through Christ's blood. When we maintain a pure heart before the Lord, we stand in His imputed righteousness, pure and holy in the eyes of God. How can we know that our garment is clean? Spend time in repentance for our own failures and sins before we begin to intercede for another's failures and/or sins. In living before the Lord we must keep our hearts pure of rebellion and idolatry. In doing so, we can be confident that our *linen robe* will stay intact and clean, free from offense before our Father. After Jesus completed the teaching on the garment of the intercessor, He closed by saying: *"Nita, tell My people everywhere how beautiful they are to Me when they come before Me in intercession for the needs of others, and those things that are upon My heart!"*

—— ✦ ——

9/83 A VISION

"OF HELL"

I saw untold thousands standing at the mouth of the lake of fire. Suddenly I saw a huge hand come from behind them and sweep them down into the fiery caldron below. I heard such screams of anguish as they fell into that place of eternal torment. Moans and cries for help were heard as they were engulfed by their eternal grave. I wept and wept as I saw them reaching out for a hand of mercy, their faces filled with anguish. Then Jesus asked: "will you endure the suffering for these?"

This is the price of a person who refuses to answer the call that is on their life. Souls who may have accepted Christ had they heard the Gospel will be ever locked in hellish torment throughout eternity because the one who was destined to bring them to Christ refused to submit to the call and be God's mouthpiece. It's a horrible price to pay, isn't it? Some might argue that Jesus would not let that happen. If a one person will not tell them about Christ, another will. Jesus will see to them. Read Ezekiel chapter three, and let the Bible answer this quandary in your heart.

——— ✦ ———

10/83 A VISITATION.

"TO BE IN THE LIGHT AS JESUS IS IN THE LIGHT."

I was lying in bed when I saw Jesus walk up to me and take my hand. He was totally engulfed in the light. This light was so bright I could hardly bear to look at Him. But, as He took my hand, I became clothed in the same light. It clothed me and filled my soul with radiant efficacy. As the light filled my soul I came into union with my Savior where I could walk the rest of my days.

It is a picture of something to come for those who will pay the price to enter in.

——— ✦ ———

10/83 A VISITATION

"THE POND AND THE UNION"

I was standing by a pond outside of the city of Zion. This pond was inviting at first glance, but it was filled with sharks, so it devoured anyone who was silly enough to jump into it. I would stand there and watch people come out from Zion and dive into this pond to go swimming. As I knew that it would cost their lives to swim in this pond, I would desperately try to warn them not to dive in. I would share with them that the pond was filled with sharks, but they would just laugh at me and jump in anyway. I would weep over the loss of their lives but could do nothing to save them. This continued for a great while, when at a lull time when no one from Zion was near the pond, I overheard the pond make some new plans. I could hear its thoughts. It said: "I am tired of just devouring those from Zion who are stupid enough to come and swim in our waters. I have decided what I will do. I will rise up and overtake Zion devouring the whole city."

When I heard this, I panicked. I ran through Zion and realizing that I didn't have anyone who would listen to me, I continued on until I had come out the other side of the city. Being alone and distraught, I sat down on the side of the curb and began to weep before the Lord. I cried out to Him: "Lord, the pond plans to rise up against Zion and overtake the city and destroy Your people." With tears streaming I cried unto Him with all my heart. Then Jesus came to me. He was hovering over me as I wept before Him. When I realized that He had come near, I looked out over the city of Zion and noticed that the pond had already began to rise into a tidal wave that was by now approaching the city. So, I looked at Jesus and wept the louder, "Lord look at what the pond is going to do. It is rising into a huge tidal wave and plans to overtake the city of Zion and destroy it!" The Lord's response at first seemed to have nothing to do with my plight and the plight of Zion. He said: *"Nita, come and be in Me."* I replied feeling a little puzzled: "I can't Lord You are God, I am only human." With that I began to cry out to Him more greatly.

I looked up over the city once again hoping to see how far the tidal wave had moved and gauge how close it was to the city. "Lord," I cried: "the pond is rising into a mighty tidal wave and is going to overtake the city of Zion. Lord it wants to destroy your people!" Jesus looked me straight in the eyes and again said: *"Nita, come and be in Me."* I shook my head and said: "Lord I cannot, You are God and I am only human. Please Lord," I continued with the matter at hand. "The pond Lord, it is rising into a mighty tidal wave." With that I glanced back at the city of Zion to see where the tidal wave was, and was horrified to see that it was moments from being at a crescent at which time it would descend upon Zion destroying the people of God. I looked back at Jesus in a panic and cried again, thinking that perhaps He didn't understand the desperateness of the situation. "Jesus, the pond has risen up and become a mighty tidal wave and in only moments will be descending upon Zion destroying Your people, please come and save them." The Lord's response was immediate: *"Nita, come and be in Me."* This time before I could dispute His words, I was lifted up off the ground and made one with my Savior! We had become so one that you could not tell Jesus from me, nor me from my Lord! I looked at the tidal wave and realized that something needed to be done now or never, as the wave was at its crescent. I blew at it, simply blew at it with all my strength. The gale that came forth from my mouth was so powerful that it blew back and destroyed the tidal wave in a moment's time.

Jesus then said to me: "this is what is meant by this scripture" *So [as the result of the Messiah's intervention] they shall [reverently] fear the name of the Lord from the west, and His glory from the rising of the sun. When the enemy shall come in like a flood, the Spirit of the Lord will lift up a standard against him and put him to flight [for He will come like a rushing stream which the breath of the Lord drives] (Isaiah 59:19)* This is soon to come! Those who will have gone into union with the Son will be His weapons against the enemy and putting him to flight just when he was sure that he had effectively destroyed Zion. Praise His name!

—— ✦ ——

3/84 A VISION

"THE END TIMES"

I had been studying the book of Galatians in the Greek hoping to get a deeper understanding of it. Toward the end of months of study the Lord awakened me every night for five nights and would teach me through visions the reality of this book. Most of that teaching has become so integrated into my Scriptural thinking that I can no longer remember what He gave me. There was however, one night that He awakened me and taught me that I can distinctly remember the things that He revealed.

I am crucified with Christ: nevertheless I live; yet not I, but Christ liveth in me; and the life which I now live in the flesh I live by the faith of the Son of God, who loved me, and gave Himself for me. (Galatians 2:20 K.J.) While in a trance I saw myself lifted up off the earth, traveling through this murky film which I was later to understand was the curse of the Law; a curse which was levied upon the earth by God as a result of Adam's sin: upward I moved until I reached heaven and the Lord's throne of rule. Then I felt myself enter right into Christ to rule with Him from His throne. As this happened I underwent an incredible metamorphosis. My mind and my soul were totally altered to see things from His perspective.

Galatians 3:13 says: *Christ purchased our freedom [redeeming us] from the curse (doom) of the Law [and its condemnation] by [Himself] becoming a curse for us, for it is written [in the Scriptures]. Cursed is everyone who hangs on a tree (is crucified).*

While in a trance, Jesus revealed to me in a vision that the word (for) could have been translated (above) and that both are correct. We would not want to omit the word for or above either one, for both are significant. He was made a curse on our behalf; therefore we must say that He was made a curse for us. On the other hand the following is also true.

In a vision, I saw Jesus lay down above the earth. Then the curse; being the curse of the Law which surrounded the earth like a cocoon was then put upon Him. He then divested this curse of all its power, after which He arose triumphant.

Following the first vision, the Lord then gave me another vision, I saw myself being lifted up off the earth until I passed through a curse which consisted of what appeared to be a fine mist, vapor or cloud-like substance. This curse was like a cocoon around the earth. Having passed through it, I was now above it and could see everything in a new light. It was as though my whole inner-man had gone through a metamorphosis. Seeing all things new, I was able to understand how to effectually deliver others from the power of the curse. So, I took a deep breath and jumped off my plateau back down under the curse to deliver others. I would bring one after the other back up through the curse, thereby setting them free, as I was now free.

This, Jesus shared with me, is His goal for every Christian. He desires that we allow Him to take us through the process of totally delivering us from the world. Through this means, He is then able to lift us up above the curse to rule and reign with Him. As this metamorphosis occurs and we become experientially seated with Him in heavenly places, we see all things through His eyes. From this vantage point we are able to understand how to effectively deliver others out from under the curse. A powerful revelation!

—— ✦ ——

5/84 A VISION

"WAR WITH CHINA"

I was with some Chinese students in a room in Los Angels, California talking about the Lord. Suddenly, they darted out of the room and into the open air. I followed them, all of us in a panic. We stood and watched as bombs fell along the coast as far as we could see. It then began to rain. I knew this rain was in fact nuclear fallout. It rained like I have never seen it rain. We just stood there in shock, and I knew it was already too late to warn anyone! I wept.

———✦———

5/84 A REVELATION

"HUMILITY"

I was seeking to write the chapter on humility for my book, "Victors Wreath". I decided to seek the Lord's face to see what He would have me write, as I felt so inadequate. I was in prayer when the presence of the Lord's humility began to flow into the room. So abundant was this sweet presence that I was compelled to lay face down before Him. As I did, He came into the room. I laid at His precious feet, clinging to Him weeping uncontrollably with such love for Him I thought I would explode. As I wept, my heart continued to move deeper and deeper into humility. I became filled with mercy, such a tender and compassionate feeling toward humanity. I wept and wept with such love and mercy for all. I felt so unworthy to even fasten His sandal upon His foot. To gaze into the perfect loveliness of His face ever again seemed too great an honor for such as I.

After about 45 minutes, He finally spoke to me. But His speech was not in words as much as in picture form. He gave me a vision of a treasure chest full of various riches, graces and treasures of the Kingdom. The treasure chest was absolutely beautiful, not because it was so pleasant to the eye, as it was not. It was very plain and even a little rugged as though it were very old. It was a chest you might find in someone's attic. But, to the heart it was so beautiful and desirable. It seemed to have another worldly glow about it. I greatly yearned for it. The treasures it held in its bosom were even more beautiful, and far more desirable, if that could be possible than was the chest. They all glowed with such splendor and glory that they were breathtaking. Then Jesus spoke to me saying: "Humility is like a treasure chest that bears the greatest gifts, graces, and riches in the kingdom of heaven. Seek it eagerly. Strive for it with all your strength for there is no greater grace than this." Then He imparted to my heart as a gift, the chapter on humility for my book and left.

—— ✦ ——

5/84 A VISITATION

"THE BROKENHEARTED."

I was siting at the window weeping while overlooking the lake. I had been through a series of storms that had left me feeling totally devastated and brokenhearted. As I wept, I was praying. I was asking Jesus to in His mercy come and heal my broken heart. The pain I felt was so unbearable that my heart physically hurt all the time.

Without any warning at all, Jesus appeared to me. He stretched forth His hands and spoke to me so tenderly. "Nita, " He said, *"You don't have to ask Me to heal your broken heart."* He was standing real close to me so I could see every line of His face. His eyes, so beautifully blue, were filled with such love and compassion, it would beggar description. As I looked deep into my Savior's eyes, it was like looking into eternity. His eyes were so filled with love that although they were solid like yours and mine, they looked like two pools of liquid love. Pools of eternal liquid love come to heal my breaking heart. My heart just melted within me. I could feel such compassion emanating from Him that an incredible peace began to flow down over me. I felt the words coming from Him: *"Nita, I want to heal you more than you could ever want it. Trust Me."* I felt such great peace and comfort come to me from my Master, that I began to feel so sleepy I couldn't stay awake. My whole being had entered into a supernatural rest. As I looked upon Him whom my soul adores, the reality of His completeness began to fill me. My Savior is utterly complete. He lacks nothing. To find my completeness in Him is to truly be complete. A person needs nothing outside of our Savior! We will never understand His completeness however until we become one with Him and He has filled every longing of our hearts with Himself alone. *[That it might develop] until we all attain oneness in the faith and in the comprehension of the [full and accurate] knowledge of the Son of God, that [we might arrive] at really mature manhood (the completness of personality which is nothing less than the standard height of Christ's own perfection), the measure of the stature of fullness of Christ and the completness found in Him. (Ephesians 4:13)* (emphasis authors)

When all that was conveyed that Jesus came to convey we parted company and I went to bed. As it was late at night, I had the best night's sleep that I had had in a very long time. Even when I did awaken for a moment, I found that I was still cocooned in His gentle love and peace. When I arose the next morning that horrible pain was gone.

The one thing that stayed with me from this visit; and it is for this reason that I share it with you; was His intense desire to heal His broken hearted children. It deeply hurts our Savior to see us hurt. He bears a pain so deep and so real when He sees us suffer that He wants with all His big eternal heart to heal us.

I might mention here that most of the time when the Lord comes to me; we do not communicate with our mouths. Most all communication goes on spirit to Spirit. For this reason, when He communicates to me, I receive not only the understanding that would take place in talking with our mouths, but I feel with my whole being, His emotions and His motivation. For instance, when Jesus was communicating His love for me, His love emanated from His whole being, into my whole being. This is the way we will be communicating in heaven.

———— ✦ ————

7/84 A VISITATION

"LOVE WILL NEVER FAIL!"

I was very concerned about someone that I deeply loved. I wanted them to know and feel confident in my love; yet, I didn't want them to think that I approved of their current lifestyle. I was in a quandary; I didn't know what to do to strike the balance. Consequently I stayed awake most of the night in prayer, seeking the Lord as to what course I should take with this person. Near dawn, I finally became so tired I began to fall asleep. Just as I entered into that place of not being awake, but, not yet being fully asleep, Jesus awakened me by speaking audibly to me.

"Nita, this is love; you search the deepest part of a person's soul until you find the most wretched thing about them. At that place, love them enough to be willing to die for their well being. Then, love will never fail."

This is My commandment: that you love one another [just] as I have loved you. v13) No one has greater love [no one has shown stronger affection] than to lay down [give up] his own life for his friends. (John 15:12-13)

I have done my very best to live by this principal and the more I live by it, the more I learn of its power. As I shared what the Lord told me with the person for whom I was so concerned, they said: "if God would say that then I want to serve Him too."

———✦———

10/84 A VISITATION

"THE JUDGE OF ALL THE EARTH"

I was still traveling with another woman at this time and we were going to be ministering in a fairly large Church on this Sunday. We were at Church and engaged in the worship portion of the service. I was thoroughly enthralled in worshipping my dear Savior, when I suddenly felt compelled to open my eyes. As I did, I saw Jesus come into the sanctuary. He came in through the ceiling and hovered over the heads of the people. I watched in amazement and awe as He came in.

He was sitting on a throne that looked like it was made of some kind of white marble or some such substance. I had seen Him sitting on this throne before, so I recognized it. He was adorned in an exquisite white robe. This robe was not like any one I had seen Him in before. It was ornately woven and inexpressibly beautiful. Over it He was wearing an ornate, golden girdle that shined with the glory of the Lord. It looked somewhat transparent and the glory shined out from within the fabric of it. He had an ornately decorated, golden crown upon His head that also shined with the glory of the Lord. Again, it looked somewhat transparent; therefore the glory shined out from within it as well. The glory shined with such brilliance, that it made the crown look like a cross between gold and silver. So, I surveyed it intently to discern what it was actually made out of. His hair was snow white, and as I gained the courage to look into His eyes, I realized that His eyes were flames of fire. It was with great pain, and fear that I looked into His eyes. For He terrified me. I quickly looked away and sought to survey the remainder of the sight of my holy King who was now before me. As I looked at His hands and feet, I saw fire under His skin, so that His skin looked like bronze set in the fire. Again, I was terrified. I had never seen Him like this before.

I wanted to look at Him, as He was a majestic and beautiful sight to behold. A sight so beautiful, I had never and I am quite sure will never again see anything to compare this side of heaven. But, I was so terrified of Him that I found it incredibly difficult to gaze upon Him. I wanted to worship Him, yet all I wanted to do was lie at His precious feet. I wanted to speak to Him, yet I was terrified, lest He speak to me. I loved Him more than words can say, yet I was totally incapable of expressing it for fear of Him.

Finally, He spoke to me. He told me of the future of the Church I was ministering in. His analysis of the future brought me great concern. Then He began to share the end of things. For this I was pleased as I saw that the immediate suffering would give way to a powerful outpouring.

Before Jesus left, He gave me the understanding that the whole Church would be going through this type of sifting, but that it would end in the bounties of God being poured out. Jesus is truly Lord of His Church. He knows how to bring down the pride of man so that He can bless us. How I love and respect Him.

——— ✦ ———

9/85 A DREAM

I had been staying alone in a cabin seeking the Lord day and night for several weeks when He spoke several things to me; one of which is the following:

1). Our military must be increased, not decreased, as we must be ready for an attack.
2). Our leaders must be supported in prayer in an unprecedented way.
3). God wants Christians in government.

———— ✦ ————

11/85 A DREAM

"COMFORT FOR THE FAMILY"

War is soon coming to America. I know that God will put a supernatural covering over those who are truly living a holy life. But, my family members, aside from my daughter and her family, are not living holy lives that are satisfactory to the Lord. Consequently, I began to grow very concerned for them. I wondered what the Lord would do concerning them. So, He gave me a dream.

My whole family was under my tent. I looked out and saw a "black cloud" approaching from Russia. As it passed over America, it destroyed everything in sight. Yet, my family was safe under my tent. When I awoke the Lord gave me; Prov. 14:11 and Josh. 2:12,13,18,19.

If we are living pure and holy lives, God will set our families apart for special protection and care during troubled times if they will come in under the safety of our homes.

———— ✦ ————

1/86 A VISION

"HEALING FOR THE NATIONS."

I was in prayer when I saw a nail scarred hand begin to rise up off the earth. Through the nail hole in His lower wrist, I saw oil begin to pour out over the earth. Soon this oil was flowing in a steady stream. As it flowed down upon the earth, it flowed until the whole earth was covered with it. The cry then weld up inside me: "Oh Lord, healing for the nations." I wept for the nations in deep intercession for a very long time.

——◆——

1/86 A VISION
ANOTHER VISION OF "HEALING FOR THE NATIONS."

I was studying the Word when suddenly I saw a vision of a king's golden staff. At the top it had a golden crown. A hand lifted it up high above the earth. Then oil began to stream forth from the top of it. It flowed like a fountain in every direction, spilling down of the earth. The oil continued to flow until the whole earth was covered with the oil from this golden staff.

——◆——

1/86 A VISION

"ISRAEL'S HOPE"

This morning in worship, the name of God became so holy I could no longer utter it with my lips. So holy was His name that I wept and wept. Then I saw a vision. It was as though Israel was becoming an extension of the Lord Himself. As this union was completed, Israel then became so holy, so sacred to God, I felt unworthy to touch even the least of His Jewish people. I felt such love for the nation that I wept and wept for a very long time.

——◆——

"AN EYE"

I fell into a spirit of travail as I was given a vision. It was as though I was looking through this huge eye that seemed as big as a mountain. I could see thousands of people in darkness. They were looking around without understanding. I knew only tears would wipe away the darkness, but the eye wouldn't cry. I wailed and wailed in such deep agony for the lost, I would have given my very own soul to save them from hell, so great was my pain for these lost souls.

Then the Lord gave a poem. Which I entitled "Who Will Weep For Me?"

Who will weep for Me?
Can't you see, can't you see?
My soul is bruised and broken
for those who are Satan's token?
He took them in war
In anguish, without the Door

Will you weep for these?
Will you fall to your knees?
Weep that they might be free?
I gave my blood, will you weep?

Weep away their blindness
In Christ's love and kindness
Weep until they're free
To spend eternity with Me.

———✦———

1/86 A REVELATION

"WATERFALL OF DIVINE LOVE"

I was in worship when suddenly I felt my heart shatter as though someone had broken it like the breaking of fine China. I wailed in deep pain. I cried: "Lord, what is this; what are You going to do?" He tenderly responded: "Nita, if you will let me do this to you, I will give you this!" Just then I felt a waterfall that felt like Niagara break through my heart. It was a waterfall of divine love. So intense was this love for every human soul that I would gladly have given my very life for the needs of anyone. This love was filled with joy, bubbling up joy that made the sacrifice a sacrifice of pure joy to give. I felt more alive than I ever have in my entire life, as it was as though I had been filled with Christ Jesus Himself.

I said: "Your will be done Lord, it is as you desire, but I hold You to the promise." He then let me know that this breaking was necessary for any one who would enter this kind of love. Our flesh must be crucified with Christ, if we are to live with Him in divine love on this earth.

—— ◆ ——

3/86 A VISITATION

"A VISIT FROM AN ANGEL"

I was lying in bed still in prayer after a long and wonderful service that night in Church. The Lord had visited us in a glorious way, so I was thanking Him for His wondrous care and mercy toward us. When suddenly the Angel of the Lord appeared to me. It seemed as though he was flying across the ceiling of my hotel room. But, the ceiling that he was writing on was much longer and wider than the one in my room. He was large, well built, and most glorious to behold. The room filled with the presence of God, and I was wrapped in a holy and reverential fear. I lay quietly and watched him for a long time, as he moved from one end of the ceiling to the other, then across its width, back and forth drawing straight lines. It seemed that it took him nearly 45 minutes to complete was he was doing. When he was nearly finished, the ceiling had a checker work of lines running across it made of light like you might see in a laser show. I finally got the courage to ask him what he was doing. His response was quick and to the point: "I am drawing lines of demarcation and division in my church." He then went about finishing what he was doing then left.

I lay pondering the sight before me and the angel's words. For, as he spoke to me, my spirit knew all that was not said. I knew that these lines of demarcation and division would establish those who wanted to go on with God from those who did not. The boundaries would be drawn in people's hearts. As people who wanted to go on with God began to move ever deeper into Him, those who did not would stagnate or worse yet, go backwards, hence lines of division would become apparent.

The next morning the gal that traveled with me mentioned that she was unable to sleep that night because she heard voices singing coming from my room. Further, said she, there was an intense, bright light coming from your room and shining into my room through the windows near the ceiling. She wanted to know why I was up that late worshipping the Lord and why I couldn't have used a smaller light as it was so late. I then told her about the visitation I had been granted. I shared with her that the light she was being troubled with was not my own as I had only a small night light on. But, the light was from the angel, for when he appeared in my room, he lit up my entire room with the glory of the Lord.

—— ✦ ——

1/87 A VISION

"THE GLORY AND WRATH OF CHRIST JESUS"

I was looking up into the heavens when suddenly I saw the King of Eternity, Christ Jesus streak across the mid-day sky in such glory that terror struck my heart. I wanted to hide from His majesty. His holiness filled the heavens, and I wanted to run, but for love of Him, I wanted to stay and be clothed by His majesty. His glory was so bright, that it was blinding, so I had to close my eyes for just a moment. When I reopened them, He was gone, and the heavens were normal.

A few minutes later, I looked at the heavens again, thinking about what I had just seen, when I saw the wrath of the Lamb streak across the heavens like lightening. However, in His wrath, the heavens were again filled with His majesty, glory, and radiant holiness. So great was this awesome sight, that I bowed to the ground in agony. I wanted to run and hide, even cry out for the very mountains to fall upon me to hide me from the wrath of the Son of God. While glory filled His great face, so did wrath and vengeance. Although, His precious blood saved me, terror of Him in His wrath was so overwhelming I wanted to die. I have no words to describe the awesome justice, and the fury of His vengeance that I saw in His face. The terror that went through my heart caused my heart to melt. I had no strength left with which to want to live. Yet, I was born again. After I was able to re-gather myself, I thought, if it did this to me, what will it do to the unbeliever when Christ comes in His wrath?

The Scripture then came to me: "*For just as the lightening flashes from the east and shines and is seen as far as the west, so will the coming of the Son of man be. V30) Then the sign of the Son of man will appear in the sky, and then all the tribes of the earth will mourn and beat their breasts and lament in anguish, and they will see the Son of man coming on the clouds of heaven, with power and great glory [in brilliancy and splendor].*" (Matt. 24:27&30) "*Then the kings of the earth and their noblemen and their magnates and their military chiefs and the wealthy and the strong and [everyone, whether] slave or free, hid themselves in the caves and among the rocks of the mountains. And they called to the mountains and the rocks, fall on (before) us and hide us from the face of Him Who sits on the throne and from the deep-seated indignation and wrath of the Lamb. For the great day of His wrath (vengeance, retribution, indignation) has come, and who is able to stand before it?*" (Rev. 6:15-17)

— ✦ —

2/87 A VISION

"JESUS WEEPS FOR AMERICA"

In an open vision, I saw the Lord bringing His people to a greater solidity in their faith. Then, the body was thrust into a time of great turmoil. This was for the purpose of purging the elect. Then I saw Jesus standing up on a mountain. As He looked down over America He wept audibly as He spoke to America prophetically.

He cried: *"Would that you had known personally, even at least in this your day, the things that make for peace (for freedom from all the distresses that are experienced as a result of sin and upon which your peace — your security, safety, prosperity, and happiness depends)! But now they are hidden from your eyes. For a time is coming upon you when your enemies will throw up a bank [with pointed stakes] about you and surround you Jerusalem and shut you in on every side. And they will dash you down to the ground, you and your children within you; and they will not leave you one stone upon another, [all] because you did not come to progressively to recognize and know and understand [from observation and experience] the time of your visitation [that is when God was visiting you, the time in which God showed Himself gracious toward you and offered you salvation through Christ].* (Lk. 19:42-44)

Then my Master left, leaving me weeping for a great period of time. I wept and wept for America. How foolish we are to think to trifle with the goodness and justice of the Lord. How could I help but weep over my beloved America.

12/87 A DREAM

"TAKE THE CITIES FOR GOD"

I saw teams of people driving up to various cites in motor homes. They would stay in parks and in people's homes. They would go out every day, knocking on doors, and into the streets preaching the Gospel, and by this means would take the cities for God. I saw many different teams in many different cities. It was part of the coming move of His Spirit.

———— ✦ ————

1/88 A DREAM

"MARK OF THE BEAST"

In a dream, I saw a woman pull up to a booth outside of a multi-layered parking enclosure. She asked for a parking ticket which would enable her to park in the enclosure. Instead of the usual parking attendant, a man was standing in the booth that required that she show the international mark on her hand before she is allowed into the enclosure. The woman in the car said: "the usual attendant has not required any such thing, not even yesterday when I was here." The man in the booth grunted: "that was yesterday, today, you do nothing without that mark."

So that no one will have power to buy or sell unless he bears the stamp (mark, inscription), [that is] the name of the beast or the number of his name. (Revelations 13:17)

———— ✦ ————

2/88 A REVELATION

"A GREAT SHAKING"

I saw another great shaking in the body, accompanied with such scandal. In spite of this however, there would be an increase in the salvation of the lost. He is going to move both severely and ever so gently in the midst of His people as many top Christian leaders are revealed in light of their scarlet lives, and subsequently brought down.

——— ✦ ———

5/84 A VISITATION

"GOD HATES SIN"

My daughter Ricci had gone to Hawaii with me to minister. One night shortly after we arrived on Maui, Ricci was in her room, just laying on her bed and praying. She had just been put through a tremendous amount of pain through a friend and was still trying to work through things in her heart. As she lay praying, the angel of the Lord came into her room. He stood in the corner of the room speaking to her. Because of the glory that surrounded him, he lit up the corner of the room where he was standing, so it was quite easy for her to see what he had come to show her.

He had something that looked like a chalkboard, upon which he wrote: God, hates sin, but He loves people. This he wrote three times; God hates sin, but He loves people. By this she understood, that she was to hate the person's sin, but keep her love even for this person, pure. But more than this, that vision was for the world.

He then gave her an amazing teaching out of the book of Hebrews, then left.

——— ✦ ———

3/88 A TRANCE

""REIGNING MONARCH OF THE CATHOLIC CHURCH"

I was to speak at a Church on the island of Lanai the following day. Consequently, I flew over to the island the day before and was entering the threshold of the pastor's home when the spirit of travail overtook me. The pastor quickly led me to my room; I climbed onto the bed, and was thrust into such travail that I was totally subject to the Spirit's agony. Unexpectedly, I was lifted up into the heavens where I saw the great beast Aligar. I had seen this beast once before in a dream wherein the Lord spoke to me about the Catholic Church. But, now I was face to face with him. He as yet was not aware of my presence, so I quietly watched him.

In appearance, he was utterly huge. I have no way to compare his size with anything as he was looking down over a cloud, so was not next to anything with which I would be able to accurately judge his size. But, I can honestly say that he was utterly gigantic. As he is the reigning spiritual monarch of the whole Catholic Church one can imagine that he must be one of Satan's highest principalities. As a rule the higher they are in rank the larger they are in size. So, one can imagine that he must be close to 20 ft. tall or even larger. I know his head was huge, and his shoulders were several feet across. He remotely looked like the Himalayan Big Foot. He stood uprightly like a man, but was covered with brown fur like a bear. His face was leathery like a bear's nose or an ape's face. Further, his face looked like that of an ape except it was flat like that of a man's. His hands were shaped like a bear's paw, with huge talons for nails.

As I quietly watched him, I saw him looking down at something, so I tried to ascertain what it was with which he was so preoccupied. I would look at him then again try to see with what it was that he was so engaged. Finally, I was able to see it. It was planet earth. I saw him moving his finger across the earth, running first from the northeast corner to the center. Then he would move from the southeast to the center, then from the northwest to the center, then from the southwest to the center. This he would do repeatedly. So, again I tried to determine what he was directing. I looked as intently as I could until I was able to see that it was people. He was directing millions of people. He was directing them to come from the four corners of the earth to the center. These millions of people were silently following his direction, walking like zombies with their right hand held out holding an idol. I continued to watch and was utterly shocked to see as these people one by one would come to the mouth of a huge hole and throw these idols in, after which their souls would follow.

When I realized that their precious souls were following the idols into the hole, I felt that I had to know what in the world the hole was. So, I kept asking the Lord to show me as I peered ever more intently trying to see into the hole. Suddenly, I saw it; it was the lake of fire. I gasped! I looked back at him and noticed written over his head; the *spirit of compromise,* and on his chest was written; *THE BEAST!* Immediately, I stood uprightly and shouted as loud as I could to make sure I got his attention. "Aligar, let go of your captives!" I was furious! Well, he saw me and heard me all right. He was angered that I dare to interrupt was he was doing. I did not care; I cared only about the souls I saw under his power. So, I shouted again, "Aligar; release your captives, now!" With that we entered into what turned out to be about a forty-five minute wrestling match over those souls. Then I was returned to my room. I was exhausted but victorious!

I later came out of my room and shared with the pastor what had taken place, to which he said nothing. I then explained that I was going to share what had happened in the service in the morning.

I was not aware that the island I was on was about 98% Filipino. Nor was I aware that the entire Church was Filipino. I only knew that I was to share what had happened, which I did. After the message, I invited any that would like to turn away from their idols to come up front and get rid of them. The whole Church responded. They forsook the idols that afore-time they would not let go of regardless of the incessant pleadings of the pastor to the contrary.

Why am I sharing that experience now? I saw the spirit behind the BEAST of Revelation. Further, he is the one with whom we must contend to liberate Catholics from their deception so that they can be totally free to serve Christ.

——— ✦ ———

4/84 A VISION

"CHINA AT WAR"

A Japanese soldier was privately showing me the target areas along the California and Texas borders that China and Japan planned to hit when they came to war with the United States. They would hit us suddenly and without warning. I cannot remember many of the target areas, but this is what I do remember. In California, it would be Modesto, San Francisco, and Los Angeles. In Texas it would be San Antonio and Houston.

—— ✦ ——

6/88 A VISION

"THE STOCK MARKET CRASH"

I saw myself siting in the living room in a friend's home and chatting with the wife. Suddenly the husband came running into the room, shouting: "the stock market has crashed, if you have any money in the bank, you can get it out right now with a card. But that opportunity will not last long, so you better do it now."

With that we all went to watch the television to see what was happening. Jobs for top executives were running across the screen at $12.00 ~ $15.00 ~ $25.00 a week. They would of course, be taken as soon as they would appear.

My friends were ministers. The wife said, well my husband and I can get roles in the movies, singing, acting and such. Just then we were interrupted with a phone call for me from the head of a leading Church denomination. He said: "Nita, Its happening just like you said it would. The market has crashed. Oh," He continued, "It's going back up ~ Praise the Lord. No ~ its going back down! It's gone! I could here the heaviness in his voice, and thought to myself, yes, it is going to be rough.

Like everyone else, my head was spinning, but I decided to stay in the ministry. So, I rose up and began to look for ministry opportunities. My pastor friend wanted to stay in the ministry but his wife wanted out because she wanted security. I couldn't much blame her, but when I thought about the sheep of God, my heart broke. I felt they needed solid ministry leaders that wouldn't desert them when they saw the wolf coming, at this time more than ever.

——— ✦ ———

8/88 A VISION

"THE BODY"

I was studying the book of Ephesians when suddenly I saw an open vision of Jesus. His body became compartmentalized. Each compartment represented a ministry in the body of Christ, all of which made up the totality of His body. These positions and who would fill them had been determined from the foundation of the earth. As each new soul was born into the kingdom, they were put in their place in Christ's body as He stood before me. Each was destined to fulfill their God-given part from the beginning to the end of time. My heart became filled with Christ's love. I felt how it was in His great love that He did this. I felt His great longing that we would rise up as His body and set our hearts to meet the needs of a needy world.

——— ✦ ———

3/89 RICCI'S VISION

"TREACHERY IN GOVERNMENT"

A dying friend came to her. He told her that he had been exposed to too much radiation at the government's hands. He said, "They are through with me now, so they sent me home to die." Then she saw a television screen suddenly appear. Faces would appear on it, one by one. As soon as the government was finished with them, they would be sent home to die. When they would die, their face would simply disappear leaving only a white silhouette on the screen. This would symbolize either their death or removal.

——— ✦ ———

3/89 A VISION

"SUBLIMINAL MESSAGING"

Ricci saw how the government was forcing the media to use subliminal messaging on many shows, advertising and the news. These messages were very dangerous, as it was an effort to control the public's thinking. He further showed her the apathy of the Church toward this dangerous masking, and how emphatically protective the government is about this practice

——— ✦ ———

4/89 A VISION

"JESUS ON A WHITE HORSE"

I saw Jesus riding a white horse and His name was The Word of God, and on His thigh I saw the name inscribed, King of Kings and Lord of Lords. He was riding with great pomp, leading His army out to war. With great valor in His heart He was riding leading out to the victory of the ages. Then the Holy Spirit spoke to me: "You can find this in Revelation 19:11."

"And I saw heaven opened, and behold a white horse; and he that sat upon him was called Faithful and True, and in righteousness he doth judge and make war. His eyes are flames of fire and on his head were many crowns; and he had a name written, that no man knew, but he himself. And he was clothed with a vesture dipped in blood: and his name is called The Word of God. And the armies, which were in heaven followed him upon white horses, clothed in fine linen, white and clean. And out of His mouth goeth a sharp sword, that with it he should smite the nations: and he shall rule them with a rod of iron: and he treadeth the winepress of the fierceness and wrath of Almighty God. And he hath on his vesture and on his thigh a name written, King of Kings, and Lord of Lords. (Rev. 19:11-16 K.J.)

——— ✦ ———

5/89 A DREAM

"666"

I saw little "666s" indicative of the anti-Christ messaging being released subliminally through all secular television and radio programming. It had tremendous power to affect your thinking.

——— ✦ ———

6/89 A DREAM

"HARASSMENT AGAINST MINISTRIES"

I awoke trembling so badly I couldn't stop long enough to even write down what I saw for a long time.

I saw a terrible demonic harassment that had set itself against ministries. Then I saw hundreds of people, ministers and non-ministers alike, those whom I knew such as family members and friends and those I had never met, those who lived by the Gospel and those who did not, being tossed to and fro in a great shaft of darkness as though they were being tossed by a great wave of the sea.

Evil spirits possessed many, others were simply being tormented. Suddenly a shaft of light beamed through the souls and spirit of those being tossed in this great shaft of darkness. This shaft of light was from heaven, and was powerful enough to free all those being tossed by this shaft of darkness. It freed these tormented souls through enlightenment producing within their hearts a wisdom that enabled them to know how to overcome. As they became free they would rise up like a mighty warrior and would burst through the shaft of darkness that had held them bound.

The people who walked in darkness have seen a great light; those who dwelt in the land of intense darkness and the shadow of death, upon them has the light shined. (Isaiah 9:2) And in that day shall the deaf hear the words of the book, and out of obscurity and gloom and darkness the eyes of the blind shall see. (Isaiah 29:18) In that day will the Lord guard and defend the inhabitants of Jerusalem; and he who is [spiritually] feeble and stumbles among them in that day of [persecution] shall become [strong and noble] like David; and the house of David [shall maintain its supremacy] like God, like the Angel of the Lord Who is before them. (Zech. 12:8)

— ✦ —

6/89 A VISION

"CROSSES ON THE RESERVATIONS"

This morning in prayer, Ricci had a vision of Crosses going up in Indian reservations all over America. In front of each Cross stood the Holy Spirit protecting His work in the reservation.

— ✦ —

6/89 A VISION

"THE WARRIOR"

In prayer today, I saw a vision of a charging warrior. He was riding a white horse, and carried a torch. The fire from the torch was blowing in the wind as he rode on. Both horse and warrior were totally dressed for war and were clothed in light. The Holy Spirit gave me to know that this is the warrior that is soon to be released in the Church. (Zech. 10:3)

— ✦ —

8/89 A VISION

"THE TREASURE"

I saw a vision of a bin. It looked like a coal bin coming up on a track out of a dark and descending tunnel. It was however, filled with vast and magnificent treasures. So magnificent were these treasures of darkness that I wept uncontrollably. As I wept, I began to see that the treasures were saints. I saw how each one is distinctly connected to the other in a vital and living connection as part of a family. Yet, it was as though they were part of the same body and under the same skin. This was a covering that glowed with the light of heaven. As this bin fully came to the surface, it entered into my heart and became a part of me. The Lord then spoke to me saying: *"I give you this treasure of wisdom, a great treasure of My kingdom."* And *I will give you the treasures of darkness and hidden riches of secret places, that you may know that it is I, the Lord, the God of Israel, Who calls you by your name.* (Isaiah 45: 3)

——— ✦ ———

8/89 A VISITATION

"THE ARMOR OF GOD"

I always spend my days in prayer and in the Word when I am on the road ministering. This allows me to be fully prepared for each service. During a time of seeking the Lord for services I was conducting in Oklahoma, an angel of the Lord appeared to me. He was gloriously arrayed in the armor of God as revealed in Ephesians the 6th chapter. His military garb shined with the glory of the Lord!

Immediately after he arrived, he began to adorn me with this vital armor. He started with the helmet of salvation, calling it by name. As he did this the helmet entered into me and fit upon my soul. Next, he announced the breastplate of righteousness and so on. Each item he spoke entered into me, to fit upon my soul. When he was done, I was fully clothed in the armor, and felt as though I was in the fortress of God Himself. I felt so protected inside this invincible fortress.

I felt as though my very being had raised up into God. I felt a confidence, power and girding up of my inner-man such as I had never known. This was not a self-confidence, or pride, or any such thing. It was an impartation of God Himself. When the angel had finished girding me thus, he imparted the understanding of how to appropriate the armor of God on a permanent basis. It isn't as we have been told in the past. Now I have written a book about it, entitled: "Putting on the Breastplate of Righteousness." (Ephesians 6:11-17)

———— ✦ ————

8/89 A VISITATION

"THE COMPASSION OF CHRIST"

I was on my way back to Oklahoma City, where I would turn in my rented automobile and fly home to Fresno. As I was driving down the Interstate, I was weeping before the Lord. I was sharing with Him how much I loved Him, and how that I wanted to be a vessel of gold for His honor. I was stating how that I wanted to be willing to suffer anything I had to go through for that to happen in the end, but my faith was shattered. I didn't feel I had the faith to walk through my heart's desire because it was so broken. 1989 was turning out to be the most painful year of my life. I was watching as my daughter and grandbaby were being systematically destroyed by a system that was established to help situations such as she unwillingly found herself in. Every time we went back to court to fight to have her little baby protected from her abuser, the abuser gained more rights to abuse. It was a living nightmare. I had already been through so much in the previous several years, that the current situation seemed to be my undoing. Yet, I wanted so badly to please my Savior. I wanted to endure through to the end of His purpose, and couldn't find the strength in Him to do it. As I poured out my heart before Him, I wept volumes of tears that seemed as though there was no end.

I was not expecting Jesus to come to me, but in His infinite mercy He did just that. He came right into my car, sat down and wept silently beside me. By that time I was weeping so hard I couldn't seem to contain myself. I told Him, "It hurts Jesus!" He just sat there and quietly wept with me with His eyes fixed on mine. When I could finally pull myself together, I tenderly asked Him why He was crying. As you see, to see Jesus cry is one of the most painful experiences I have ever had. It is like watching your little child cry with intense pain. You love Him so much you would do anything to heal the reason for His tears.

"*I weep for your pain, Nita*" was His gentle response. "*I remember the pain of this iron furnace like it was yesterday.*" He continued. I looked at Him in amazement. "*In fact, I wear the pain of this place every day.*" I looked at Him in shocked amazement and cried: "How? Jesus, I don't want You to hurt like I am hurting. I love You!" Now my heart was ripped with a new kind of pain. A sudden pain that felt overwhelming to me. "How, do You wear this horrible pain?" I again questioned, searching His gentle eyes for some sign that I had misunderstood Him. He again tenderly replied: "*Nothing passes into the life of one of Mine, that it does not first pass through Me. I bear the pain before it ever comes your way. Then when you suffer, I bear your pain right along with you.*" "Oh, no!" I cried. "Jesus, I love You so much, I don't want You to ever suffer the way I hurt right now, please!" He looked at me with such compassion it would beggar description, and He said: "*Nita, I would have it no other way!*" I just looked at Him, I was feeling the love He had for me and could see in His gentle eyes how much it meant to Him to identify with my pain. I just didn't know what to say.

Just then, He began to show a little smile. Then, He leaned over and looked deep into my eyes it felt like His was looking deep into my innermost being. Then He sat back just a little, and said, while still looking at me very intensely: "*Nita, thank-you for being willing to suffer for Me.*" At this point He began to smile. His smile grew, and grew until His entire face was radiant with glory. Again His said: "*Thank-you for being willing to go through the pain of the process of being made an instrument of gold for Me.*" By now it looked as though I was seeing heaven in His wonderful face. I could see how much it meant to Him, I could feel how much it meant to Him that I was willing to suffer in order to obey Him. To see Him smile with such radiance meant everything in the world to me. It made everything I have ever gone through to answer the call upon my life worth the price I have been asked to pay.

I shared this remarkably personal visit with you to say, Jesus cares! He must allow our suffering, but it matters to Him when we suffer. He is not indifferent to one little bit of our pain while living in the iron furnace called earth.

Isaiah 63:9 Says it like this: *"In all their affliction He was afflicted, and the Angel of His presence saved them; in His love and pity He redeemed them; and He lifted up and carried them all the days of old."*

—— ✦ ——

8/89 A VISION

"THE ART OF NECROMANCY"

I saw evil spirits take absolute possession of people's minds. I say absolute, as the spirit dominated the person's personality. It was not just a possession of the flesh, but of their innermost being, of their will. Once being so possessed, the person would then send other evil spirits against Christians. These spirits would desperately try to gain control of the Christian's minds, and ultimately gain entrance and possess the will. We were able to withstand them by using the name of Jesus. Near the end of this warfare, I saw a memo come across the bottom of the screen: "This is the art of necromancy."

—— ✦ ——

8/89 A VISION

"THE COMING WAR"

I saw a convoy of evil spirits being sent out against the church. This was a major demonic task force. I would equate them with the Green Beret of our own national Air Force. They were a special task force with higher authority and power than what has typified such demons in the past. The main spirits were such as perversion, fear, pride, lust, dissension, depression, guilt, rebellion, greed, delusion, and deception. They were ordered to attack Christians, weaken and finally overtake them by possessing them and uniting their fiendish personality with their own.

I saw spirits visit people in dreams and non-threatening visitations leading them through a process of delusion until they were at the mercy of their evil intent. I saw them teaching people from as early as three years of age to adulthood how to work with them and eventually how to become possessed by them. These will deceive Christians and non-Christians alike. The only way to be safe from them and keep your children safe is to live a holy life, get wounds healed and walk in forgiveness staying under the blood covering.

—— ✦ ——

8/89 A VISION

"A WORD FROM THE THRONE"

While in intercession Ricci was taken up before the throne of the Lord. Sitting before our Lord's throne interceding on behalf of revival the Lord spoke to her thus giving a promise of four things that would take place in revival.

1. Wonder working power in our spiritual life.
2. Wonder working power in relationships.
3. Wonder working power in healing of body and emotions.
4. Wonder working power in our finances.

"So," said He, "sit at My feet and receive the teaching of the Word just as Mary did and obey all that you hear."

Ricci

—— ✦ ——

10/89 A DREAM

"ABOUT CURSES"

Ricci had a dream of people involved in witchcraft that have little specialty and boutique shops wherein they make and sell things such as sculptures, arts and crafts sort of things, paintings etc. Before they sell them, they put curses upon them, so that when the buyer takes them home, they bring that curse into their homes to begin to work its insidious work against that family.

———✦———

10/89 A VISION

"REVIVAL AMONG THE JEWS"

I saw virtually thousands of Jews getting saved in coffeehouse type ministries. This was particularly true on the East Coast.

———✦———

11/89 A VISITATION

"THE VINE THAT GOES OVER THE WALL"

I was climbing a huge brick wall, not as you would think by crawling up the wall, but I was walking up the wall in an erect posture, fully intending to go over it. All the way up this wall, the enemy chased after me desperately trying to stop me from going over it. With each step I took, I could hear and see what was happening in the spirit world. Each step I took resounded with the sound of thunder as I put my foot down. Once I began to climb up the wall, I could see crater size holes being made in the spirit world with each new step. I was doing great destruction in the enemy's camp; this was why he was trying so desperately to stop me.

Finally, I reached the top of the wall. The minute I did, I saw Jesus standing there waiting for me. Upon seeing me reach the top; He immediately lay down on the top of the wall. Then He said to me: "*Today your vine has gone over the wall and I have become redemption to you.*" I felt the redemption enter into my innermost being. Then He disappeared.

Jesus is our redemption the day we are born-again. However, the power, and value of this redemption is not fully appropriated and experienced in its highest form and truest reality until we have fully overcome the world, the flesh and the devil. Upon this victory we are then ushered into the true adult sonship experientially. The covenant for which we have been sealed is then opened to us and we are granted our inheritance. All this happens this side of heaven for those who go over the wall as Joseph of Old Testament renown did. This means we have been totally removed, severed from the spirit of the world, and although we still mobilize on the earth, we are walking only in the Kingdom of God free from any identity with Satan's Kingdom. This reality is effected by the actualized crucifixion of our sinful nature, a work of divine grace. The soul upon this crucifixion is considered to have actualized his death with Christ in whom he is then raised in Christ and now reigns with Him. The soul now free of the sin principle is free to become the residence of Jesus. He is no longer just living in the Christian's spirit, but has taken up actual residence in the saint's purified soul. In this the Scripture is fulfilled; It is no longer I that liveth, but Christ that liveth in me. Galatians. 2:20, Genesis 49:22-23

— ✦ —

11/89 A VISION

"SATAN A RAGING LION"

I was awakened out of a deep sleep by the sound of a roaring lion. When I awoke, I saw Satan hovering over me looking like a mature male lion. He was roaring in fierce hunger, and a savage craze for blood was in his heart. I could feel his lustful and savage hunger. It was consuming me. Feeling desperate, I asked the Lord whom it was that Satan wanted with such a savage hunger. My little grandbaby was sleeping in the bed next to me with her mother, my daughter. The Lord responded: *"Tiffany, follow My instructions and you will protect her."* He then told me what to do giving me instructions that we promptly obeyed.

Why am I sharing this with you? Because Satan hungers for all our children in this same manner. But, we can protect our children from his insanity by obeying the spirit's prompting, and living a holy life, maintaining a prayer life, covering our children with the power of Christ's blood, and finally bringing them up in the love and admonition of the Lord.

Be well balanced (temperate, sober of mind), be vigilant and cautious at all times, for that enemy of yours, the devil, roams around like a lion roaring [in fierce hunger], seeking someone to seize upon and devour. v9) Withstand him; be firm in faith! (1 Peter 5:8 & 9)

———— ✦ ————

11/89 A VISITATION

"JESUS, FAT WITH TRUTH"

I had experienced the Father asking me on three separate occasions over a period of a year and one half, if I would like to know and love Him as Jesus did while here on this earth. Upon the third occasion I finally had the faith to say to Him, that if it were really possible that I could have such a relationship with Him, I would certainly want it and would pay any price to have it. It was in response to my answer, that I would be experiencing the following two visitations.

I was in a time of worship, when Jesus appeared to me. He was fat with truth. In fact, He looked about 500 pounds fat. But, it was His spirit that was fat. He was fat with the living truth. I could sense what was going on inside of Him as He stood before me. He was the living Word, personified and incarnate in the flesh. He was filled with an effervescent joy, peace, love, and faith. He was the very persona of the fruits of the Spirit. (Proverbs 28:25 & Isaiah 10:27 Amp.)

He then told me to come and stand next to Him, which I did immediately. As I stood next to Him, His Spirit enfolded mine. All the passions of my fallen humanity began to abate, and in their place I was filled with His passions, nature and character. The Scripture reveals in Galatians 5:22 & 23 the fruits or nature of the Spirit. It was this nature that filled me. No words can express the wonder of what I experienced. He gave me revelation on several Scriptures. For instance, He shared that what I was experiencing at that time with Him was what the Holy Spirit was referring to when He inspired John to write John 1:14. Further, it was out of His fullness that we have all received His great blessings. This is what John was stating when he wrote in John 1:16 that we have received out of Christ's fullness a great abundance of blessing. What are the potential blessings? Union with Christ, with Him living the fullness of His life through us, just as I experienced.

— ✦ —

11/89 A VISITATION

"THE KINGDOM YOKE"

I was in prayer and it was now four days after the last visit by my dear Savior. I was praying a prayer that I had prayed every day for two years. I would open the Bible to Isaiah 11:2-5 and read it right out loud. Then I would say: Father, I know that this Scripture is foretelling the office and ministry of the coming Messiah. But, in my heart, I want this for me so badly. If I am wrong in wanting it, please forgive me. But, on the other hand, I am going to keep asking you for it until you either tell me that I am wrong or you say that I can have it."

With that I looked up and saw Jesus standing in front of me. He immediately told me to come and stand next to Him. I arose as He commanded and stood next to my Savior. As I did, a double yoke bar such as you would put upon two heads of oxen appeared upon His shoulders and then came and set upon mine, so that we became double yoked together.

As this yoke set down upon my shoulders all my human passions began to disappear. Not only my emotions, but I became totally incognizant to my own existence. I knew that I was there, but yet, at the same time I was incognizant to my own existence. Once emptied, Jesus Himself stepped right into my soul. It felt like He had opened me from the back and stepped right in. He was thinking through me, He was feeling through me. Then Jesus spoke, saying: *"Nita, you have been praying the Scripture in Isaiah 11 for two years, asking Me to impart that to you. This that you are now experiencing is what you have been asking Me for. This is the Kingdom Yoke as recorded in Isaiah 11. When I was here on earth, I would call out to people: 'Come unto Me, all ye that are burdened and heavy laden, and I will give you rest. Take my yoke upon you and learn of me; for I am meek and lowly of heart: and you shall find rest unto your souls. For my yoke is easy, my burden is light. and take my yoke upon you.' (Matt. 11:28-30) I was indeed concerned about Judaism, as it had become little more than a yoke of slavery over My people. However, that is not what I was referring to, when I made the invitation. I was referring to the yoke of the sinful nature. Nothing is a greater burden on the soul of man than it is. It seeks only carnal pleasures and hinders the soul from ever reaching up into its God. Right now you are free of the tyranny of the sinful nature and in its place you are wearing My yoke. It is indeed a yoke of freedom. Would you like to live here?"*

"Jesus," I said, "You mean it is possible for a human being to live here?" He responded in His usual tenderness: *"Nita, would you like to live here?"* Jesus, if You are saying that I can have this, You know me, I will pay any price to have it, I will give whatever You require of me. Yes, I want it." *"All right then you shall have it,"* was His response. He proceded to give me awesome revelation about other scriptures, then was gone. I was left to marvel at what had just happened.

My Dear Friends, my mind was no longer my own, it was the mind of Christ. I have longed and yearned for my Savior with such an intensity sinse the day I was saved. But, at that moment, I no longer yearned for

Him, for He was inside of me, filling my soul, completing me. I felt wholly complete for the first time in my life.

One more thing; before He left me in both of these visitations, He told me that anyone who will, could have this place in Him. Anyone who is willing to pay the price can have this place of refuge in God.

————✦————

12/89 A VISITATION

"THE SPIRIT OF BABYLON"

I was preparing to head up to Washington State for a couple of different meetings. One would be in a Church, the other with Y.W.A.M. So, at this time I was in prayer particularly over the Church in which I was going to minister. Suddenly, a great demonic prince appeared in my room. I looked up at him, and before I could say a word, he spoke to me saying: "You will not come to the Northwest. I don't want you bothering me up there." I said to him: "Who are you?" He replied: "I am the spirit of Babylon, and I rule over the Northwest, and I do not want you coming into my domain, ever! Stay away from me, do you understand!"

He was a great Prince, fully clothed in military armor. He showed me the dimension of his reign that covered the entire area that we commonly refer to as the Northwest. This covered Washington State, Oregon, Idaho, Montana and Wyoming. His rule is one of great darkness. I saw a massive cloud that just hovered over the entire area, he was over it and owned the cloud. He showed this to me when he told me where he ruled. He tried his level best to radiate all the fear he could toward me trying to intimidate me. I finally just commanded him to leave in the name of the Lord. So, he left.

————✦————

"JESUS, LORD OF ETERNITY"

I was ministering at a Y.W.A.M. base in the US on: "Jesus the Son of God." I would begin to read a Scripture aloud, when the presence of God would become so strong, all I could do was lift my hands and worship Him. I had people before me who were Methodists, Lutherans, Baptists, Pentecostals and a couple who were not even saved. But, I couldn't help but lift my hands and worship Him. His presence was far too overwhelming and called for nothing but reverent worship and adoration. I was compelled to worship Him just as I was on one of my visits to heaven.

As the intensity of His presence would begin to lift a little, I would once again attempt to read the Word and teach. Then the next wave of His presence would come and we would all be in high worship all over again. Even those who were not saved were compelled to do as I was doing, worship His majesty. This happened several times. Then, without notice Jesus came into the room. He was hovering over the people, standing in all His majesty. My breath was taken from me as I looked upon Him. Suddenly, I saw all time pass before me in a linear line. I saw from the beginning of time, to the end. It passed before me, in a split second of time. I clearly saw scenes of Adam and Eve leaving the garden, Abraham's life, of the Tabernacle, and of the wilderness wanderings under Moses. I saw the era of Queen Esther, Daniel, and the Babylonian captivity, the time of Jesus' ministry on earth, and the final exile of Israel from the land. I saw the Pentecostal outpouring and the Church move from the Jew to the time of the Gentile. I saw the dark ages in the Church, and the Reformation. I saw Nations rise and fall, right up to this present day. Then I saw the future, the great outpouring, the rise of the anti-Christ, and the destruction of nations. It all moved past in me in a moment's time, but with clear definition, telescoping right into our Lord's belly.

As I followed it, my focus was riveted upon the Lord. He then became a little transparent, and in His belly, the New Jerusalem appeared. It was so beautiful, so glorious; I began to weep as I stood there in awe of what was before my eyes. This city was alive with a golden glow. It was the most beautiful thing I have ever seen. I just stood there gazing at it. The power and holy presence of God was in the room where I was standing so magnanimously, that I later wondered how I could have continued to stand. It was some time after He left that His presence began to lift. But, we experienced an awesome move of God that day in miracles, healings, and deliverances. (Colosians 1:20 & Hebrews 1:2-3)

12/98 SIX VISIONS

I woke up to six visions today, one right after the other.
1. Hell is hungry and after the Church.
2. New authority coming to the Church.
3. Jesus will make streams in the desert and the wilderness a fruitful place for the Church.
4. Bounties from the hills coming to the Native Americans, as they give their hearts to Christ.
5. God going the heal the tears of many generations among the Native Americans.
6. Again, another warning about the persecution of the Jews in America

12/98 TWO DREAMS

"OLD NATIVE AMERICAN RELIGIONS"

I had two dreams about the Native Americans. First I saw Satan trying to hinder what God was going to do among the Native Americans by infiltrating the tribes with the New Age Movement.

In the second dream, I saw an old Native American woman build a resort type of place. It was a beautiful log cabin lodge. She would bring

Native American leaders and those who desired to be Shamans to this lodge to teach them the old Native American religions. For this privilege they were to take the practices back to their tribes and win many converts. Because of her own powers she was able to support the movement with much satanic power. By these means she was determined to bring the old religion back to one of acceptance and prominence. Further, I saw that she would be successful.

As to this dream, I didn't necessarily think that this was an actual event that was going to occur. Rather, that it is an indication that the spirit of occultism was going to court these people among the tribes and would succeed. Yet, that will not stop what God is going to do.

———— ✦ ————

12/89 A VISION

"THE PRACTICE OF IDOLATRY"

In a vision I saw a priest walking up a few steps to an altar made of hewn stones. It was a rather large and elaborate altar. I immediately remembered that this elaborate altar was not acceptable to God, therefore He had given specific instructions in the Old Testament for an Israelite not to use such altars. So, I asked Jesus what the priest and the altar was all about. (Exodus 20:25-26)

The Lord responded to my query with: *"This is a priest who is now going up to make a sacrifice on a strange altar."* I asked: " To whom is he making this sacrifice?" The Lord responded: *"To himself!"* "To himself?" I replied. *"Yes,"* answered the Lord; *He is making an offering to himself as his god."* "What altar is this Lord?" I again queried. Jesus responded: *"It is the altar of unforgiveness. When a person refuses to forgive someone who has offended them, they are in effect building an altar of sacrifice to themselves as their own god. The unwillingness to forgive is rooted in self-idolatry."*

———— ✦ ————

1/90 A VISION

"THE DERELICT"

I had a vision of an old homeless man tumbling down a hill. His clothes were ragged and dirty. He himself needed a bath, as he was very dirty. When he reached the bottom, he just sat there, hopeless and forlorn, feeling totally worthless.

The Lord then said: *"This is how Satan wants you to see yourself. It's an attack against your righteousness. He hates your righteousness and is very jealous to steal the power of it. Don't let him!*

I was going through a great battle at that time, as I already previously mentioned. Due to the suffering we were enduring for my granddaughters sake. We had lost a lot of critical battles for her protection, and it left me feeling hopeless and of no value to the Lord. For this reason, He gave me this vision. But, it is a word for many in the Church. If you are living a holy life, Satan will attempt to discourage you and steal the power of your righteousness for warfare. The Lord's word concerning Satan's attacks? "Don't let him!"

———— ✦ ————

1/90 A WORD

"NOTHING CAN HURT YOU IN ME!"

"Nothing can hurt you in Me ~ be not afraid of calamity and ruin. No outside force can hurt one of Mine. Only self can cast shadows on the path of life in Me. Notwithstanding, be afraid of the spirit's unrest and the soul's disturbance. When the heart once again sings and the rest restored then all is well.

"When the calm has been broken ~ come, be alone with Me. Make immediate discovery of the heart's breach with its rest in the Vine. When rest is broken, those evil forces who daily surround the righteous child are able to find openings through which they sling their painful darts to cause much havoc. In

My rest, is the heart's safe dwelling. So, don't tarry, run with all fervor to your hiding place in Me and keep your rest secure."

——— ✦ ———

1/90 A VISION

"TWO PATHS"

I saw in a vision that there were two paths to holiness. One path led you to true holiness, the other led you to false holiness.

The first path would lead the believer to an impure or false holiness. This path was fairly smooth, and had a rather dim light that surrounded it. Outside of this lit area were large and foreboding trees that hung over the path, blocking out most of the light.

This impure holiness is where most of the church walks, if they walk in any kind of holiness at all. People quit smoking, drinking, and partying when they get saved, and begin to walk in greater cleanness in their life style. They quit swearing and so on, and learn to talk the 'Jesus talk.' Some will even quit listening to secular music, in turn listening to only Christian music. Some will even begin to help out in Christian work, or endeavor to answer the call that is on their life. There are also those who will begin to develop a Word and prayer life. They will study the Bible, and even spend time in prayer every day. But that is where it all ends. The Gospel never enters the heart to the point of changing the deeper things such as pride, gossip, murmuring, anger, and the like. For that reason, though they may be very good people, they will always remain in an impure holiness. The road on this path is much smoother, because the devil will not contest these people as much as he will those who want to move on in God.

The second path, had even less light on it, but I could see that it was full of chuck-holes, and it was rocky, also there were a lot of protrusions in the path, making it very difficult to walk down. This is the path of true or pure holiness. Only those who really want to go on with God will walk down this path. The reason there is very little light on this path, is that it is not used much. For the believer to walk down this path, the light must come from their heart, as the trees greatly overshadow the path therefore keeping insincere seekers off the path.

Those who walk this path, have gone beyond where those who walk the former path have gone. The Lord deals with deep-seated areas of sin on this path. The more earnest the believer is about their quest in God, the deeper the probe will go until the Lord purifies them to the point that He is able to crucify their sin nature, at which time Jesus will come in to take up residence in their souls. On this path Jesus will eventually not let even the most minute sin go without dealing with it. It is a walk of tremendous discipline. But, at the end the seeker is walking a walk of pure and undefiled holiness, which is most pleasing to the Lord. The attacks of the enemy are much heavier the further one walks down this path, however, God uses this high intensity walk to bring greater and faster purging in the heart of the willing seeker. So, although it is by far a rougher path, the inner glory is equally more magnificent. So, might I add, is the relationship with our Lord! This path is therefore highly cherished by our Father, as are the believers who are willing to walk down it. (Jer. 6:16)

———✦———

1/90 A WORD

"THE NEEDS OF CHRIST"

"Many know the needs of man; but, few know the needs of Christ!"

———✦———

"SPIRIT OF VALOR"

"The spirit of valor is wrought at greatest strength in meekness. Though at times I allow a crushing ~ keep a trusting heart. Face all your difficulties at rest in My grace, undaunted in My love and you shall never fail in any task I set before you.

"Let nothing that others do to you alter your treatment of them. Your task is to tenderly love your brother, and with earnest and compassionate care for his deep inner needs. Leave the training and discipline to Me. As you walk in this way, no circumstance, person, or devil shall ever defeat you. For love will keep you held firm in the spirit of valor paving the way to sure victory!"

———◆———

1/90 A WORD

"LOVE IS"

I was on a walk by myself when the Spirit of the Lord began to speak to me. He would first speak a sentence then let me feel what I was being told in a baptism of His Spirit. Following are many of the simple one line statements He made, they were about 5 minutes apart;

"Nita, love is generous. Love is always kind. Love is bounteous in its display of care–love is easy to please. The smallest kindness, the smallest gift, the most simple act of mercy is generously received by love. Love is careful in its concern for others. Love is gentle in its treatment of others, friend or foe. Love finds great pleasure in the most simple demonstrations of reciprocity. Love never ceases in its joyous giving. Love delights to forgive."

I was utterly lost in His Spirit by the time He finished His communications to me.

———◆———

1/90 A VISION

"ALTARS OF IDOLATRY"

I saw hundreds of people crouched down in little individual altar rooms they had made in the hills of Seattle, Washington. Still people were flocking to Seattle in droves to make their own altar rooms in the hills. What they were worshipping were altars dedicated to idols of self. Over the city was a spirit who was calling out to people everywhere, to come and build altars to idols of self, and they would find peace and prosperity.

— ✦ —

1/90 A DREAM

"THE FAT SHEEP AND THE LEAN SHEEP"

I was given a dream to explain the difference of the spiritual vision of a teacher vs. a prophet. In it I was talking to a teacher of the Word. As I spoke to him, I was looking out over the ocean and could clearly see a hurricane approaching. With it would come a great flood. The Inn in which we were residing for this conference would soon be swept away and with it would be the loss of all the Lord's sheep that were with us.

I cried out to the teacher: "Mark, we have to tell the people about the hurricane and coming flood ~ can't you see, it's already almost too late!" Mark turned to look out over the ocean to see what it was that I was clamoring about. What he saw, I was able to see. The ocean was calm, and there seemed to be no sight whatsoever of any storm.

"Mark", I cried: "We have to warn the sheep and get them to safety before its too late!" With that, I looked out over the ocean once again, and spotted some fat sheep grazing on a grassy ledge over-looking the ocean. I cried: "Mark, look at the sheep, they will be swept away if someone doesn't rescue them." We both turned to look at the scene together, and once again I could see it through his eyes. Everything was calm, and placid. One could see the possibility of an approaching storm, perhaps a little spring storm, near the horizon. But, it seemed to be nothing to be so concerned about. Mark then turned to me and said in a rather irritated tone: "Oh we've got plenty of time, don't worry about it."

I could see the water beginning to rise, and felt desperate to save the fat sheep on the hill. It was obvious that my friend, the teacher, was going to do nothing to assist in this emergency, as he didn't perceive that there was an emergency. So, I ran downstairs to get out the door and jump into the by now dangerously rising tide, as it was by now the only way to get to the fat sheep. I tried desperately to swim out to the sheep, but to no avail. Thoroughly exhausted from swimming against the incoming tide, I lifted my head up at one point and saw the fat sheep still grazing on a high ledge, and thought to myself, if I don't give up, perhaps I can still reach them in time. Just then a huge wave raised up and crashed over the cliff, taking the sheep with it back into the ocean. All hope was lost. Now broken and stunned, I turned around and began to swim back toward shore, hoping to get to the Inn in time to save the remaining sheep.

As I arrived, soaked and utterly exhausted, I found Mark and the very lean sheep at the Inn preparing to leave. Mark had just started to escort them to a place of safety. I began to hurry everyone along, knowing that if they moved quickly they would still make it, but I wondered at the apathetic way my friend, the teacher was at his task of protecting these vulnerable sheep.

The fat sheep are those who gorge themselves on the Word, but still live and gorge themselves on the world. They will be swallowed up by the coming storm.

The lean sheep, are those who have taken the Word seriously and have cleansed themselves of the world living by righteousness alone. They will be brought to safety right on time. (Ezekiel 34:16-22)

———— ✦ ————

2/90 A VISION

"JESUS, MERCIFUL SAVIOR"

In a time of great crises, many in the body find themselves debilitated by the voices of their past, telling them they are of no value and that God would have no reason to help or save them in their trouble. These voices are silent, but trouble the soul stealing it from its desperately needed rest in God, nonetheless. By silent, I mean they cannot be heard by the ear, but the heart hears them ripping away all sense of value when the person needs it the most.

Well, the Lord spoke to me in a vision about this. First, He said: *"It isn't the enemy that is always to blame, your soul is your biggest problem."* In other words let Jesus heal you of your past wounds and the voices will lose their effectiveness.

Then came the vision: It came in the form of a visual letter. This letter was being typed out by a computer as the Father spoke the words. Further, I could see pictures that would depict the reality behind His words of comfort.

"Jesus being just, righteous, holy, and merciful, willingly came to earth, giving up and leaving behind such glories. (I then saw the glories of the Son, prior to His coming in the form of a man.) He, being God gave full expression to His deity, majesty, and splendor. He abode in such majesty and splendor as can never be beheld by the eyes of mortal man. In His supreme deity, angels worshiped Him. All creation was established in His essential being. Every created thing was subservient to Him and He reigned in righteousness.

"The heavens were arrayed in golden and glorious splendor by and through Him. Much in His joy, He reigned in full glory right by My side, delighting in the sons of God. His heaven where angels roam and saints find delight in the fullness of life, is a place of infinite peace, love, joy, and beauty where no evil foe can enter. Of all that He had, His greatest fulfillment was found in the glory that He shared with Me as part of the eternal Godhead.

"He left all this, humbling Himself and was found in the form of man. He humbled himself still further, and walked as a servant among men bearing the ridicule, the scorn, and the reproach with which wayward men treated Him who hated and deplored a holy God as their government head. He was misunderstood, and despised by the very ones He came to save in righteousness. He humbled Himself still further, and bore the sin of all mankind, going through the death that was both humanly painful and humiliating. He died the death of a traitor to His people and a convict, an outcast to His generation; although in reality, He was sinless and the divine

Healer of those to whom He was sent.

"To this Jesus willingly submitted and with earnest desire He embraced all that He endured, for you! He left the glory He had with Me and embraced such agony, that He might grant to you the glory of sonship and heavenly bliss. All that is His, He has given to share with you. The joy of His holy habitation is now yours throughout eternity. His intimate fellowship as a Son with His Father, He has now paved the way for you to experience, even now as one of My own. All power and authority was given to Him, and with His own, He longs to share it for the good of all.

"So now:" The Father continued: "this is yours through My Son. So, put My Son around your innermost being. Adorn your soul with Him. Clothe your innermost part with My Son, and all He has for you, will be yours experientially."

When His awesome presence lifted and the vision came to an end, I was left cradled like a babe in the arms of a loving father, clothed in His peace. I felt like I was resting on a cloud of abundance where neither fears, nor foe could assail. For the next nineteen days my prayer partner and I were visited with the fragrance of the Lord in prayer and throughout the day.

Dear Reader, the price that our Dear Savior and divine Friend paid, He paid for all who call upon His name. He willing paid this enormous price that He might give to all who are willing to receive, the glories that are His to share, today and through eternity. I thereby want to encourage you to do as the Lord instructed me to do, and make yours what Jesus so wants to give.

———— ✦ ————

1/90 A VISITATION

"A TRUE BOND-SLAVE"

I was in prayer, when Jesus came into the room. He told me to walk over and kneel down in front of Him. As I obeyed Him, and was kneeling down in front Him, He put His hand upon my head. The minute my Lord's hand touched the top of my head, something wonderful happened. All of my human passions began to fade away. Simultaneously, I began to be filled with my Savior's passions. His humility, meekness and love filled every part of my being. I cared nothing about myself. I cared for His will. What He wanted—I wanted, and I would have gladly given my life to obey and fulfill His perfect will. I thought about traveling to a distant country to preach the gospel. I thought; oh, that is a dangerous country, the chances of coming out alive are not at all good. But, no matter, if my Master and Lord is pleased for me to give my life there, then I am pleased. If He would be pleased to bring me home safe, then that too is fine, as long as He is glorified. That, my dear soul, is all that matters. With that thought, I was filled with great joy! Then the following Scriptures came to my mind, bringing even more comfort and joy: Sacrifices and offerings You have not desired, but instead You have made ready a body for me to offer. Again; Behold, here I am, coming to do Your will O God~[to fulfill] what is written of Me in the volume of the Book. As these verses filled my heart, I was further filled with the joy of sweet surrender to my Master.

Then Jesus said: *"Nita, this is where Paul lived. When he said that he was My bond-slave, he was speaking of a place that he had come to in Me. A place where nothing matters except My will and bringing Me great glory. Would you like to live here?"* I quietly said: "Oh yes Lord. I would give anything to live here." He replied: *"Very well then, you shall have it."*

The sense of sweet surrender stayed with me the rest of the day. I also typed the Scriptures out that had been quickened to me, and put them in my Bible. It is still my desire to enter into that place with my Lord. I want to encourage you to desire it also. For any one who is willing to pay the price for such a walk, can have it. It is God's good pleasure to give us the Kingdom. Of all the things that that promise represents, none is so wonderful and important as that is.

—— ✦ ——

5/90 A DREAM

" STRONG WARNING

First: guard the children. Protect them with lots of love and nurturing. Get them in the Word and prayer, and get the Word in them. Develop them in a strong love and commitment to family.

Second dream: God is soon going to begin revealing ministers who are ruled by Satan, either because they are bound by sin, or serving him by choice.

5/90 A DREAM

"FIGHT FEAR"

I saw myself wrestling with an evil spirit of high authority. In the end, I won, though he tried desperately to kill me in several different ways before his final defeat. When I awoke, the Lord spoke to me audibly saying: *"Fight fear like the plague, for as fear increases in the soul, the standard of God decreases."*

1/90 A VISION

"THE TORCH"

I saw a vision of a huge torch on fire. The flame was both brilliant and large. This torch was moving down a direct path. In my spirit came the understanding of it. "The release of the Prophets is now at hand."

6/90 A VISION

"THE TIDAL WAVE"

I awoke at 2:00 a.m. to a vision of a huge "tidal wave" breaking through the family room window. The words, "Satanic tidal wave breaking through upon the family is on its way" were immediately released in my spirit.

I lay awake weeping and praying for the family for a long time after. In this time the deep impression was given, that we need to tuck the children into the strong arms of love and instructions about Jesus and the kingdom. Surround your children always with prayer and the blood. Get your children into the Bible as early as they can read. Ultimately God is going to release a powerful prophetic mantle upon the body for the sake of healing and restoration of the family.

(Mal 4:5,6) *Behold, I will send you Elijah the prophet before the great and terrible day of the Lord comes. And he shall turn [and reconcile] the hearts of the [estranged] fathers to the [ungodly] children, and the hearts of [rebellious] children to [the piety of] their fathers [a reconciliation produced by repentance of the ungodly]; lest I come and smite the land with a curse [and a ban of utter destruction.]*

"A VISIT TO HEAVEN"

Today I was wrapped in the Spirit in prayer and suddenly found myself walking down a lane in paradise. On either side of this lane were beautiful trees of many different sorts. As I was walking along, before long I realized that I wasn't alone as Jesus was walking with me. Shortly thereafter I noticed a lovely gently trickling stream running along side of us to our left. As Jesus continued to speak to me, He led me over to stand beside the stream. It was more beautiful than anything I had seen on this earth. It was more beautiful than the mountain streams or lakes even in Canada. The water was crystal clear so that you could easily see the river's bottom. It was crystalline blue in color, but had a texture that was somewhat different than our earthly water. The rocks in the river's bed were different as well. Instead of the ragged rocks such as we have on earth, the riverbed was full of precious stones. They were vibrant in color, but didn't clash against the rest of their environment, rather, they complimented it. Jesus instructed me that these precious stones were symbolic of His children all in various stages of growth, however each one being precious to Him. The fact that they were in the stream spoke of the fact that as His own they are covered by the waters of His Spirit being washed and prepared for the day of their homecoming.

The trees were varied in size and in variety. However, each one from the trunk to the branches, to the leaves were in perfect symmetry. The same was true of the little shrubs. I saw glorious colors and hues of green and brown in this exquisite forest of pristine beauty. The flowers were so lovely, delicate and colorful. I saw varieties and colors I have never heard of or seen on earth. They were delightfully fragrant, a bouquet of aroma that was so pleasing to the senses, but not in anyway overpowering. The many fragrances blended so beautifully, each one reminded me of my Savior whom my soul adores. The flowers formed in utter perfection and perfect in beauty each one reminding me in some way of Christ's own beauty and His own perfection. All that I saw made me only love Him more. He told me that He especially loved the flowers as they reminded Him of His own on earth. When we live holy lives our lives exuded this same fragrant aroma, and it is so pleasing to Him.

With all that I saw in paradise each scene being more beautiful than the last, none however, were as beautiful as the One who stood beside me. All of heaven bears a glow that is given it because of His own holy presence. The flowers, the trees, the water, all shine with this same glow which makes everything far more beautiful than it would ordinarily be. The Bible says that God clothes the lily of the valley. Well in heaven, one can see the beautiful holy adornment with which it is clothed; as it shines with this glory in a beautiful and vast array of colors. Still as lovely and even breathtaking as everything is, it cannot compare to the beauty of our Savior! I look into His lovely bronze colored face that is so gentle, so kind, so filled with holy love, and my heart melts. I look into His beautiful blue eyes and I see eyes that are filled with such love that they look like liquid pools of eternal love and passion for the likes of one like me. I feel cherished, comforted and supremely important to Him. When I see Him, there is always a certain heavenly glow about Him, but that is much more apparent in heaven.

When my Master speaks, His voice is so sweet, that all of creation seems to quiet itself for just a moment to enjoy the beauty of His heavenly presence. His voice seems to bring life to all that surrounds Him. Jesus rarely speaks to me with His mouth, but when He speaks, the words flow from His whole being into my whole being. I seem to sense them, taste them, feel them and understand them intellectually all at the same time. When He speaks, His words seem to enfold me and heal me of things I don't even know need to be healed. So wonderful is His voice. I don't understand it all, but I have experienced the effects of it many times. I don't ever just hear His wonderful words; I always fully experience them as they enter into me. It is by this means that we communicate by the (S)spirit. All of heaven communicates in this way. How I love Him exceedingly.

After our walk in Paradise, Jesus took me to a room that looked like a classroom. There I saw Him personally teaching a dear friend of mine the Word. I overheard the things that He said to her and felt quite encouraged and comforted by His attention to her. Then He looked at me and said to tell her what I heard and saw, for this was going to come to pass in her life. Then I was sent back to my body.

When I returned, it was quite painful to reenter my earthly abode. After entering into rest in my temple, I turned to tell my prayer partner of the things I had just experienced, when she squealed: "turn away from me, your eyes are flames of fire, and the glory is shining from your face." With that we both bowed our heads and the holiness of God descended into the room. We sat in silence for quite a long time worshipping the Lord. It was some space of time before she could look at me as it took time for the glory to dissipate. When at long last we could talk I started to share with her what had happened, she told me that she had heard my side of the whole conversation, and asked me to fill her in on what the

Lord actually did and said. After she left, I walked in the encompassing presence of the Spirit for the rest of the day.

—— ✦ ——

7/90 A VISITATION

"REIGNING MONARCH OF THE KLUE KLUX KLAN"

I was in bed, but wide-awake as I had just received a visit from heaven. Suddenly and without warning the reigning spiritual monarch of the Klue Klux Klan appeared in my room. He was quite tall, a cross between a wolf and a man and well dressed in full armor. He spoke to me, saying: "This is my territory, and I don't want you bothering me, do you understand!" Well, I knew why he was threatened by my presence here; the last time we met I ruined a stronghold of long standing of his. On the other hand, I was surprised, as I did not know that I was in any special area belonging to him. At the time I was in Augusta GA in a hotel room which had been provided by the Church I was ministering in. So, I asked him: "What do you mean?" He replied in a rather aggravated but authoritative tone: "I have power over a lot of the churches in this area and I don't want you troubling me. This whole region is under my dominion, in fact my headquarters is near here, and I want you out of here. Don't trouble me do you understand!" With that I saw what appeared to be Savannah GA as a special place of headquarters for this guy. Well, I told him to get out of my room in the name of Jesus and he left. The minute he left, I saw an animal looking spirit siting on top of the Church I was ministering in. So, I asked him what he was doing there. He replied: "I am here to stop the unity of races that this pastor wants to see take place." I rebuked him and he left. Well that turned out to be quite a night!

—— ✦ ——

8/90 A VISION

"JESUS RIDING A WHITE HORSE"

Again, I saw Jesus riding a white horse. On His thigh was written, "King of Kings and Lord of Lords." He was going forth conquering in righteousness. Again the Scriptures of (Revelation 19: 11-16) came to me, by the Holy Spirit. Then the Lord spoke these words to me. "Holiness unto the Lord"

——— ✦ ———

10/90 A DREAM

"THREE DREAMS"

First Dream: I was walking up a hill toward a building that I was going to be speaking in for a Women's Conference which was to be entitled "Women and Warfare." All the way up the hill, I saw these snakes attacking these women, which meant I had to kill them to protect the women, which of course I did. Then the Lord spoke to me from heaven saying: *"Tell all women everywhere, they need the power of the Omnipotent actively at work in them."* The next day I was invited to speak at a women's retreat, which I accepted. I almost never speak at women's gatherings as my burden is for the whole Church, not just a special group in the Church. It turned out that what I had seen in this dream was the place we would meet. The title of the conference was just as I saw what it would be, "Women in Warfare."

Second Dream: I was trying very hard to get these men to pray for a mutual friend who was dying of heart trouble. But, all they would do is give him Scriptures of comfort and encouragement. The Holy Spirit then spoke to my heart saying: "The prayer of faith will heal him." I could easily see that if he could believe and if one of these men would pray for him in faith, he indeed would be healed. But, I could not get a single man to listen to me. Then a voice spoke to me from heaven saying: *"Tell all* men everywhere that they need the power of the Omnipotent actively at work in them."

Third Dream: I was sitting on stage with three Doctors. We were being interviewed on a talk show.

The woman psychologist said as though she was responding to a statement that someone else made: "The problem with the young Indian converts is this; as soon as they are saved, the Chieftains and the Shamans seek to drain their faith through constant spiritual attacks which they send out until the converts have no strength to stand in their faith." Again, the Lord spoke to me from heaven saying: *Tell everyone everywhere that they need the power of the omnipotent God actively at work in them."*

———— ✦ ————

12/90 A VISION

"TRUE BEAUTY, IN GOD'S EYES"

First, I saw a woman who was so beautiful that she had won an outstanding award for her beauty. It was not the sort of award as would be given at a beauty pageant, but was a special award that only she had received. She was very impressed with this award. And thinking that she didn't want to disappoint those who had voted for her to receive it, she had plastic surgery to make herself even more beautiful. After this, I saw her walking out on a balcony waving at all her admirers. None were allowed to come close to her however, lest they accidentally hurt her and mar her present beauty. Her agent advised this, and she thought that perhaps it was wise advice, therefore followed it.

Then the scene changed and I saw Cyrano de Bergerac riding around on a bike in a clown's suit. He was going from door to door, giving little dolls of himself to children in the neighborhood. Each child that received one of these funny looking dolls would be so thrilled. Their little hearts would be ecstatic with joy and they would come outside into the courtyard, dancing and singing with sheer delight. The scene then came to an end.

Then appeared a black screen upon which the following words were written. *God does not see beauty as man sees it; what He sees as beauty, what brings the Lord great joy, is not outward beauty, but the beauty of the heart. For He does not look upon outward beauty. But, what is most pleasing to Him, and is very precious in His sight is a meek, gentle and peaceable spirit, a heart that is tender and filled with goodness. This is to Him a most highly sought treasure.*

— ◆ —

12/90 A REVELATION

"JESUS IS LORD!"

I awoke at about 1:00 a.m. in the morning and was unable to go back to sleep. So, I decided to spend the time in prayer. I said to the Holy Spirit, not knowing at all what to expect, Holy Spirit, please I want You to rise up within me and proclaim that Jesus is my Lord. Immediately He (the Holy Spirit) filled my mind, and proclamations began to come forth in such power I was in awe. Due to an injury I had a type of laryngitis, yet, these proclamations came forth in such power that the words from my mouth sounded like they were being spoken through an echo chamber. Words, such as *"Jesus is the Lord! Jesus is Christ for the Nations, Jesus is my Lord, Jesus is the Lord of the Heavens! Jesus is Lord of all the earth! Jesus is Lord of the eternities!*

With each proclamation, the words would echo through my head. It was as though my skull no longer confined my mind, but my mind became linked with eternity. So His words would echo through my mind, then on into eternity. All this was accompanied by a sweet pain, which made me wince. I was amazed and even a little startled. I had not known what to expect. But, what happened truly showed me the difference between the Holy Spirit saying Jesus is Lord through me, and me saying it in my own strength.

When I thought everything had settled down I got up for a few minutes. When I returned about five minutes later, I lay back down in my bed thinking I would spend some time meditating on what had just happened. But, when my head hit the pillow, I was immediately thrust back into the place where I had left off. The Holy Spirit again took possession of my mind. I told Him: "Holy Spirit I don't only want Jesus to be Lord over my mind, but over my heart, my spirit, my soul and my strength." Immediately the Holy Spirit shot down like an arrow shot out of a sling, toward my heart. As He entered my heart, He pierced my heart and His anointing exploded releasing fire throughout my heart. Further, He filled my whole being in a way I had never experienced in my life. Then in a split second I was before my Savior's throne.

Kneeling before Jesus, I was in such awe of His majesty and holiness. He had in His hands a beautiful golden crown, which He sought to put on my head. I felt so unworthy, I pulled back, not wanting anyone to be crowned but my Master Himself. He then told me to come close to Him again and He proceeded to put this beautiful crown upon me. But instead of it fitting upon my head, when Jesus put it on me, it enlarged and slipped down becoming a golden yoke upon my shoulders. I found I couldn't bear to look at Him for His holiness, so I bowed my head down to the ground, As I was kneeling with my head to the ground, I was sort of curled up. His holiness was emanating to such a degree, I wanted to shield myself from it, and be hidden for the sight of His majesty. Just then I noticed two wings come from behind me to cover me, shielding me from the holiness and majesty of my King. However, that was not enough, I still felt too conspicuous and too unprotected from that divine holiness. So, I asked Jesus to please cover me. He graciously complied and two wings came out from behind Him to further cover me. There I stayed in that position until I was returned to my room.

I began to worship Jesus from my spirit, as I felt so overwhelmed with love and adoration of Him, I was compelled. As I worshiped Him, I began to proclaim His names as they came to me. As I began to proclaim different names, what appeared to be a baby cherub would rise up and hover over me. Each one rising to a corresponding name; each one to worship the Eternal King in his own language to that name, until there were eight cherubs worshipping the King of Glory with me. As they worshiped Jesus with me, our worship rose to such heights as I have never known before. Then I could hear the angel choirs join us in worshipping the Great King, lifting us to higher realms of worship yet. Then we would move into times of adoring silence, then rapturous worship, then again into silent adoration. It was wonderful! Our worship lasted about forty-five minutes as far as I could tell. Then I was back in my room. Unable to sleep, I continued to worship my Savior for a long time afterwards.

———— ✦ ————

1/91 A VISITATION

"THE MIGHTY MEN OF DAVID"

I was at this time going through a very difficult decision making process. The Angel of the Lord stood in my room with his sword drawn for the three days that I struggled with this decision. His presence was both disconcerting and comforting at the same time. Once my decision was made, and before he left, he spoke to me about the mighty men of David. He told me how they would soon come forth, how they would be empowered and what they would need to go through in their preparation for this vital ministry. I have a tape on this subject that can be ordered. It is entitled "David's Mighty Men of Valor!"

I was told that they would be prophets of the highest caliber. Specially anointed to bring down the long-standing strongholds of Satan amidst God's people. They would be righteous judges, and mighty counselors on behalf of God's people. (Isaiah 1:26) They would bear an unprecedented anointing, for which they will have gone through an immense purging to bear. In fact, they will be those who have been co-crucified with Christ in an experiential way. They will have a godly love for authority and will bear the meekness of the Son. Finally they will have God's own love for His sheep. (Zech 9:5-7; 13:1)

They will be the government of the Lord fully restored to the people of God. What they pronounce judgement upon will be judged. What they bless will be blessed. They will be sent forth to bring down the unrepentant Saul reign with much weeping, and they will bring in the reign of the spirit to the Church.

———— ✦ ————

"APPROPRIATION OF THE THRONE"

I was taken into a trance. (Acts 10:10) Then my spirit was lifted up and seated on a throne in heaven to rule and to reign with Christ. Then He spoke to me saying: "Appropriation of the throne means identification with the family." Immediately after Jesus spoke this to me, I descended right into the middle of the family of God on earth.

In reigning, there is a certain humility and meekness required of one that is not required of those not in that position. Jesus requires a meekness and humility that will bring one in the authority of the throne to identify with the least and the lowest in the family of God. Moses was a prototype, though he ruled as a prince, he was not ashamed to be identified with his race who were but slaves.

——— ✦ ———

5/91 A VISITATION

"JESUS, THE GREATER DAVID"

Jesus came to me. First He called my name; so, I arose from sleep and responded to Him. I said: "Speak Lord for your servant is listening." He was dressed in the garb of a Jewish shepherd. Upon His head he wore a Yarmulke. His hair, instead of being long, brown and wavy as it has been in most of my visits with Him; was shorter, auburn and curly just as was king David's. As He sat before me, He was playing a funeral dirge on a clarinet. It was sad and foreboding. I saw tears lightly running down his ruddy cheeks. I asked Him why He was so sad. He immediately showed me a shield with two horns crossed upon it. It looked like a family crest. But, I knew that they symbolized the close of something. It was as though something was going to be put away. This something was of great significance to Him and brought Him much pain to have to put away. My heart became very sad for Him. Again, I asked Him what it was that was bringing Him such sorrow. Finally, He told me that He would soon have to put away those who sought to fulfill their ministry in the flesh as Saul sought to fulfill his call. This was necessary in order to bring forth the reign of the Spirit that would grace the new Davidic reign. This, Jesus does not do with joy. It brings Him much grief to have to expose and put out to pasture so to speak, those who try to fulfill the call by means of the flesh. But, the Church needs the reign of the Spirit if it is ever to fulfill its purpose in the earth. So, for that reason, He will do what must be done.

———— ✦ ————

1/90 A VISITATION

"A HEAVENLY VISION"

I was in Church on the Lord's Day, worshipping the Lord with the rest of the congregation. When I felt drawn to open my eyes to worship Him and looking upward I realized that the ceiling to the Church had been rolled back exposing the heavens. Then the heavens were rolled back and standing there looking at me was Jesus. Standing on His right and His left were Saints, behind them were angles who stood about a head taller than the saints. They were all waving at me with great big smiles on their faces. Jesus looked so joyful and friendly, I was amazed. I kept looking at them not knowing what to do. So, I kind of waved at them and smiled sheepishly. I don't know if everyone just left leaving the Lord alone with me, or what happened, but the next I knew He was all I could see. Perhaps it was just me, as when He is near He is all I ever see.

I kept gazing at Him waiting to see what would be next. Then I noticed that extending from earth to heaven was a road or path of pure light. I found my gaze volleying from the Lord to the path and again to the Lord. I didn't want to take my eyes off Him, because I didn't want Him to leave before He could communicate to me what it was He came to say. Yet, this road kept drawing me. I felt that there was something to this road or path that I was missing, that was very important, something I needed to see. At length I realized that I needed to look to the side, as something seemed to protrude from the side of the path. Looking it over

I saw that it was a crossbeam. Across the top of the path of light was a crossbeam of light. So, I took a step back so I could get a good look at it. It was a Cross of light! It was a Cross that extended from the earth to heaven. I looked back at Jesus hoping He would tell me what it was all about. He was looking with such love in his heart for the Cross. I could both see the love and feel it coming from Him. I watched Him for a few moments trying to ascertain what might be said or done next, when I saw the Father. He was looking down over Jesus and the Cross, with so much love for the Cross that it would beggar description.

At that moment I realized that the Father didn't hate the Cross. I didn't realize that deep in my innermost being I feared that the Father did hate the Cross, because His Son had been so brutally murdered upon it. The Lord spoke the Scripture; For God so loved the world that He gave His only begotten Son, that whosoever believeth on Him shall not perish, but have everlasting life. As the Lord spoke this I realized that deep in my heart of hearts where I was unaware, I thought that the Father felt like He could only love us because of His Son's willingness to bear the Cross. I was misinterpreting the Scripture. The way my heart was reading it was that God so loved His Son that He would be willing to accept anyone who would believe on Him, because Jesus died on the Cross. As the truth that it was out of His great love for me, that God sent His Son to die on the Cross pierced my heart, I began to weep. The Scripture went in as Jesus said it, not as my wounded heart was interpreting it. Such a healing took place that my heart began to explode with the glory of my Savior. I was filled with joy.

I looked back at Jesus to see what He was doing. Still I could see His heart was so filled with love for the Cross. Then He looked at me and said: *"In the days that are ahead, I am going to magnify the cross above all other things in the earth. Never before has the cross been so greatly magnified as it will in the last days. Truly"* He said: *"I will glorify the cross before the world, so that the whole world will know beyond doubt that I have come, and that I am who I say I am.* He then shared some other things with me; again the saints and angels were back; everyone began to wave good-bye to me, then they left. My heart remained so full of His glory and joy for many days. However, I must admit that whenever I thought about Jesus or the Cross, or the Father's love for the Cross, I would weep with tears of joy and thankfulness.

8/91 A WORD

"A WORD FROM JESUS"

Jesus spoke to me in a vision. He said: *"There is a purpose for each one in the Kingdom of Heaven. You can't earn a ministry, only fulfill a call. Daily faithfulness unfolds the richness of the call; it doesn't produce it. For only what is born of the Spirit is of any value."*

1/90 A DREAM

"A PROPHETIC DREAM OF WARNING"

The Lord showed me the following things in a powerful prophetic dream.

Ministries building an illegal house with the Lord's money will be brought down. By the term illegal the Lord refers to two categories.

1. The first are categorized as being those who are ministering by a familiar spirit rather than the Holy Spirit.
2. The second group are those who are committing serious infractions against the Lord's will for building their own kingdoms, and who are frivolous with the Lord's money and whose hearts are filled with greed.

8/91 A VISITATION

"THE WHITE HORSE"

I again saw the white horse that I saw in January of 1990. (I wrote about this visitation in my Book "Prepare for the Winds of Change.") This time when I saw him, he was running across America. The Lord then spoke audibly to me: *"Watch for this horse; he leads to war!"* So, I understood that his coming would preface the coming of the Red Horse that I had seen in June of 1990, as the Red Horse is the horse who takes peace form the earth.

Next Jesus told me: *"The next level of judgment begins in 1992. The separating process has begun and will soon escalate."*

——— ✦ ———

9/91 A VISITATION

"A VISIT TO HEAVEN"

I was awakened in the middle of the night and escorted to heaven by a huge magnificently beautiful Angel. I could feel myself flying up through the atmosphere and stratosphere. The pressure of the wind against my face was a little frightening, as it seemed that we were traveling at the speed of light. For that reason, I clung to my guide for fear of falling.

As we entered heaven, we slowed down, so I let go. The first thing we flew by was a factory. We flew to it then around it. It looked just like a Church building in the Jerusalem on earth. Yet, I knew it was a factory. It was a large rectangular building with golden domes on the roof. It looked more beautiful than most homes on the earth. I felt strongly impressed that they made something for homes inside of it. I saw many people walking in and out of it.

Then I was taken to New Jerusalem. It was magnificent! It was a city set on a hill. A golden city set on a hill! Many of the buildings were white, and looked like they were made of ivory. Yet, they glowed with a golden glow. Many of the buildings had various sizes of golden domes. The roofs were also of gold. There were many and various types of homes, with different architecture, and different sizes. Each one was absolutely beautiful. Incidentally, the least attractive home and for that matter the smallest home I saw was more beautiful than any home I have ever seen on the earth. The streets were virtually paved with a transparent gold, that was utterly beautiful as they too glowed with the glory of the Lord.

I saw many shops that looked like mercantile or what we might call boutique shops along the main street of the city. I saw people going in and out of them with merchandise in their hands. So, although I know there is no buying or selling in heaven, I have learned that we can procure goods that we may want or need from these little shops. We don't pay for them; we just go in and take what we desire.

People were so busy. Heaven seems to be a very busy place. So, if anyone thinks they are going to go to heaven and sit on clouds and eat grapes all day, they are very wrong. Everyone was busy about the Master's business. I had often wondered why there would be streets paved with gold, as I knew that in heaven, all one had to do was to think about where they wanted to be and they could be there. But, I saw many people walking on these streets. They were very busy, going in and out of homes or the shops or what have you. But they would walk along and talk with one another, for although they were busy, no one was hurried. Most were dressed quite casually.

Around the circumference of the city, was a most magnificent river. The water in this large river was crystalline. In fact, I kept mentioning how the waters were so beautiful, and were crystalline. The river was crystalline and shined like diamonds in the sun. They actually look like a transparent blue, mercury. The water has a different substance there than it does here. This large river was very wide and also quite deep. It was large enough to handle great ships. It reminded me of the Dalles between Washington and Oregon. As silly as it may seem, I had difficulty taking my eyes off this river because it was so beautiful. It looked like it could have gone around the whole city, as it traveled quite a distance, at least half way around the city for as much as I could see. I noticed that there were large bridges that stretched across the river, I saw bridges spaced every five miles or so. They looked like bridges that would rise for boats to go under. I realized that boats traveled this river. I knew it like I knew my name. So, I began to look for boats, but saw no sign of them. This puzzled me, as I knew that the Scripture spoke of the waters where upon no oar propelled boat could travel. I came to learn however, that the boats that traveled on the waters in heaven are not propelled by oar or motor, but by the Spirit of God. I realized that these bridges were for people to walk across to leave the city and go to other parts of heaven such as paradise, where I had been on another trip.

As I mentioned earlier, this golden city is set on a hill, so it is multi-level. I kept looking for the temple like structure that I had seen at an earlier visit. Or any kind of temple for the Lord Himself, as there seemed to be a perfect place for one right at the top of the hill. I searched desperately wondering all the time I was there where the temple was. I knew that what I had seen earlier was a meeting place for the saints, but where was the Lord's temple? Of course I realized later that the Bible says there is no temple in the city, for the Lord Himself is the temple.

The glory of the Lord shined throughout the city. The city virtually glowed with His glory in golden splendor. It was breathtakingly beautiful. Then I realized that this was the city that I had seen in the belly of my Lord in 1989, and I told the angel that. Then I repeated myself, as I was amazed as the reality of it hit me. I kept telling my escort how utterly beautiful the city was. I felt a little silly, but I couldn't help but repeat myself continually, as it was so majestic and lovely.

I thought to myself, then said, "angel I bet you are beautiful too. I bet you are as beautiful as this city." Then for the first time I saw him face to face. He was beautiful, just as every other angel I had ever seen. Only one difference, this one was of such a stature that instead of the eyes of love that I had seen in others, his eyes were piercing, filled with wisdom, and almost stern. He was a huge being and it frightened me to look at his eyes. It was at this time that he spoke the message he had taken me there to receive and then took me home. Before we separated, he told me I would be given many more visits if I remained faithful to the Lord.

——— ✦ ———

9/91

"A DREAM"

After I returned to my room, I was given a series of dreams. I will share only the last one with you, as it was a parabolic word for the Church.

"I sat down in the front row seat in front of a raised platform. I noticed off to my left, this sad bouquet of yellow flowers. Before I could say or do anything about it, a young boy about twelve years of age began to mock me. He snorted: "The yellow flowers are dying, they're all droopy! When you see it you'll cry." Then without hesitating one moment for me to respond to his sarcasm, he jumped up, went over and grabbed the flowers and brought them over and set them down in front of me. Then he looked at me and chided: "Will you cry?"

I didn't answer his question. Instead I spoke the word of the Lord to him. "It isn't for lack of water that the flowers are dying; but it is their unbelief." Then I looked directly at him and said: "It is the Lord's compassion that causes Him to cry. His heart is broken with compassion because of the peoples' unbelief."

"Unbelief of what"? You might say. His people nurture unbelief regarding the treacherous days that are coming upon the whole earth in the very near future. In addition they have a sobering lack of faith in God's goodness in tough times.

—— ✦ ——

1/92 A VISION

"THE POWER OF LOVE"

The scene opened with me sitting on a sofa in a very elegant drawing room. Across from me was a prince. It was in his home that we were conversing. He was a very handsome man, with jet-black hair, and deep blue eyes, which reflected the kindness in his heart. He was dressed in a military uniform of the "commander and chief" of his countries' military.

He was sitting across from me weeping uncontrollably. I was much engaged with trying to comfort my dear friend. He had just discovered that his wife was once again committing adultery; this being now the eighth time in the eight years of their marriage. Her paramour was always the same man. He was a wealthy businessman who traveled to their country extensively in the course of his business.

Because of their frequent interludes he had purchased an apartment in a very elite hotel where they would always meet. My friendship was not only with this prince, but with his wife as well. Consequently, I knew that she was not involved with these liaisons out of a lack of love or respect for her husband. It was, rather out of deep seated and unresolved pain. Somehow, her relationship with this man provided a temporary escape from the pain she felt incapable of dealing with.

In an effort to save the marriage of my two dear friends, I had gone to the room where she met with her lover, to talk with her privately. I talked with her at length sitting in the living room of the apartment. Looking at her curly blue-black hair tossed so perfectly around her face, her milky white skin, and violet colored eyes which where by now red with tears over the wrong she had committed against her husband who she loved more than she would ever know how to show. Truly, she was beautiful. Knowing them both well, I also knew she was as beautiful inside as she was on the outside. As I looked at her tear drenched face, I knew my insights had been confirmed. She was as broken over what she had done as her husband was for the treachery against him. But, I also knew it would take a miracle for her to ever let him know because of the mountain of guilt she now carried. We talked much as she poured out her heart, her fears and deep anxieties. I sought to comfort her and assure her that things would work out in the end.

Now, as I am sitting before this pining prince, I am so glad that I had taken the time to go and see his wife before coming to talk with him, as I now had a much better understanding of things. We are sitting across from one another, and I am watching my brokenhearted friend weeping in bitter despair. So, I begin to plead with him to hold on and to forgive her one more time. Tears streaming down his bronze face, he at last responds: "Nita you don't understand, it has been eight years. She has done this for eight years."

I wept with him as I continued to intercede with him for their love. I am feeling such love for him; I think, she is a little crazy for doing something like this to someone who loves her so much. The prince then breaks into my thoughts saying: "I should have married someone who understands love–someone like you!" Realizing that in his pain, he was attempting to run from the divine lessons he was meant to learn, I firmly, but gently replied: "Prince you both are of royal blood, I am not. Your thoughts are out of the question, so let's consider them no more. Now the truth is you love her, and she you!" I am looking intently into his swollen eyes, and again see so much pain, so I soften my voice even more and proceed with carefulness. "Prince, the key is forgiveness. Forgive her one more time. My dear friend, this will sound very hard" I gently continued: "But, I must say it. I have been to the room where they meet. Prince, to usher in the full healing of your bride, you must buy the room. Buy the room and embrace her at her sin. If you will my dear friend, you will heal your bride. Prince, I saw on the table in front of the sofa, a golden eagle just about to mount up and soar. I believe that eagle depicts you. I mean you have nearly learned the critical lessons God wants you to learn. But, to finish your course, you must buy the room. Buy the room dear Prince, and you will mount up and soar as one who has won the prize, and your bride will at last be healed."

As I spoke to him ever so gently, he continued to weep, crying out the pain of his devastated heart. He wept, but he listened, and knowing him, I knew he would do as I was encouraging him to do.

When I awoke, the Lord spoke to me audibly. He said: *"Suffering has done a thorough work, when through your own pain, you are able to move beyond the walls of self-protection and have compassion on the deep inner needs of your violator."*

—— ✦ ——

4/92

"A VISION"

Jesus spoke thus to me: *"A dream or vision given by the Lord is like a parable in the hand. Even though we may not understand it, if we will humble ourselves and pray, God will give understanding. The parable is designed to give enlightenment of truth to the true seeker, while it hides the truth from the rebellious. This is true of all parables, whether given by dreams and visions or through the Word."* (Mark 4:11-12)

I saw it in picture form as the words played out. I saw a person holding a bird in their hand as tangible evidence of the promise. As understanding unfolded, the bird was transformed into the promise itself.

———— ✦ ————

4/92 WORD

"JESUS ON THE CROSS"

I had been teaching on Romans 6-8, in a nightly Bible study. We were going through the Word by studying the Greek extract out the golden nuggets of truth. The group that was studying with me was interested in entering into the union with Christ, which is the focus of that trilogy of chapters. We were studying it in the Greek therefore studying it carefully and slowly. The crucifixion of my sinful nature was daily upon my mind, and in my prayers in an even more heightened way than normal. I must admit, this crucifixion is a central topic of thought anyway, but I was being endowed with a renewed hope in this regard through this study.

It was during this study, that Jesus appeared to me one night, waking me from a deep sleep. He was hanging on a cross. If you were to see Jesus in this way you might think or say many different things. But, what it brought out of me was a fervent desire to be co-crucified with my Savior. Consequently, that is what I cried out. From the depths of my inner-most being, I cried out to Jesus: "Jesus, crucify my sinful nature! I want to be nailed to the cross in reality! Please, Jesus I want to be co-crucified with you as Paul was!"

Jesus looked straight into my eyes and said: *"This is a worthy thing you have asked. This, the crucifixion of the sinful nature is the highest of all wars, the victory of which is the most noble of all victories."* Then I felt the cross go through my whole being like fire.

No longer on the cross, but now standing next to me, My Savior gave me a teaching. He said it like this: *"The Greek word [hamartia] used in*

Romans 6 is the same word found in Isaiah 53:5 which in Hebrew is [awon].
Both speak of the sinful nature. I was bruised as I took your sinful nature upon
myself and nailed it to the cross. You see the word wounded comes from the
Hebrew word [chalal] which speaks of the desecration of something holy.I was
the Father's holy sacrifice. I was desecrated by your transgressions that you
might be healed. Because of my great love for you I bore it all, that you might
have experiential freedom from a life dominated by the sin nature." As my
beloved Jesus spoke to me His eyes were so filled with love and joy over
having wrought this living freedom for us, that I was amazed.

"This is what is meant by Romans 8:3 & 4. For God has done what the
Law could not do, [its power] being weakened by the flesh [the entire human
nature of man without the Holy Spirit]. Sending His own Son in the guise of
sinful flesh and as an offering for sin, (Hamartia), [God] condemned sin in the
flesh [subdued, overcame, deprived it of its power over all who accept that
sacrifice], (4) So, that the righteous and just requirement of the Law might be
fully met in us who live and move not in the ways of the flesh but in the ways
of the Spirit [our lives not governed by the standards and according to the
dictates of the flesh, but controlled by the Holy Spirit]" (emphasis authors)

After Jesus left, I wept and wept in thankfulness for His profound
mercy. Later, I did a complete Bible study on all that He spoke.

———— ✦ ————

7/92 A DREAM

"THE NATURE OF THE BRIDE"

In a dream I saw a person moving about here and there living out of
the passions of their flesh. This included the pride of life, the lust of the
flesh, and the lust of the eyes which compelled them in all that they did.
It was both sad and at the same time, disgusting to watch. They were
utterly controlled by those wicked passions and felt that this was the joy
of life. I felt compassion for them.

"A VISION"

After I awoke from the dream the Lord began to speak to me in a vision. The Lord spoke saying: *"This is the way of one who would be a bride of Christ; and she shall radiate the seven virtues of Christ's bride."*

II Peter 1:3-7 (K.J.) gives us an idea of what that means. *According as his divine power hath given unto us all things that pertain unto life and godliness, through the knowledge of him that hath called us to glory and virtue. (4) Whereby are given unto us exceeding great and precious promises: that by these ye might be partakers of the divine nature, having escaped the corruption that is in the world through lust. (5) And beside this, giving all diligence, add to your faith virtue; and to virtue knowledge; (6) And to knowledge temperance; and to temperance patience; and to patience godliness. (7) And to godliness brotherly kindness; and to brotherly kindness charity.* This last word in the Greek is actually [Agape]. So, we are to add to our faith, that virtue (moral excellence) such as goodness, humility, and meekness would fit into this category. To virtue we are to diligently strive to add knowledge. We want knowledge of God and His ways. To knowledge we are to add temperance. That means self-control, or a watchfulness concerning all the passions of our flesh. We are not to govern our lives by these passions, but rather the passions of Christ. To temperance we are to add patience in dealing with God and others. This demands that a nature of meekness and humility be fairly well developed, giving us the ability to deal tenderly with the failures of others. To patience we are to add godliness, which means that we have become ensconced to a deeply entrenched life of holiness and purity. To our godliness we are to add brotherly affection. This means a love for the brotherhood of the faith. We are to have a tender and compassionate feeling for all those who are of the faith. Our brotherly affection we must finally be developed until we are walking in agape love for all mankind. This is a love that would compel you to give your life for even your worst enemy for the sake of his well being if necessary.

Don't be afraid, my Dear Reader. We don't have to come to this place of maturity in our own strength. This is something the Lord makes incumbent upon Himself to develop in the heart of the diligent seeker. We must put our will to the race, and seek with all our heart to through these lofty gates enter, but God will grant the ministry of His grace to aid the yearning believer in his journey. This is to what the Scripture refers when it says that God has given us through Christ everything that pertains to life and godliness. He has already made provision for the journey.

——— ✦ ———

7/92 A VISITATION

"THE PURITY OF CHRIST"

I was lying upon my bed, praying and meditating upon the Lord when suddenly He appeared. I was not expecting Him in any way, but I was so delighted to see Him Whom my soul so deeply loves.

We were together, but I was neither in heaven, nor was He on earth. What Jesus did, He had done before, so it wasn't new to me, He had removed the veil between heaven and myself. So Jesus remained on the threshold of heaven, yet did not seem more than four feet away from me. This is how we conversed.

Jesus had on a white gown like I have seen Him in so many times. But this time it appeared as though there was some kind of crown on His head. I would look one moment and would see what looked like a tubular crown of light. I would look again and it would appear to be a crown of thorns.

As Jesus stood before me He did what He does so often when He wants to make a statement to me that could be better expressed by letting me experience it, rather than for Him to simply say it. He began to emanate His purity in light that was so beautifully transparent. Oh, my Dear Readers I have seen His purity before and it always makes me cry for its beauty. He emanated His purity and His holiness making these two aspects of His character clear and distinct. In it I saw His utter truthfulness. I saw how there was no shadow in His lovely turning, He was truth personified. It was not in Him to tell a lie, or even to shade the truth to His own benefit. The love that was flowing from Him was so filled with mercy, that it was nearly overwhelming. I further saw, that He would in no way ever manipulate, for any reason. His love was utterly pure.

After a brief time, Jesus wanted me to see the world as He sees it. I began to feel satanic forces off to the side of me. It made the very air I breathed thick with satanic personality. The very air began to feel dirty and dingy. I felt the presence of every evil under the sun. Murder, rape, hate, rage, lying, every form of deception, trickery, and treachery were apparent. I felt the presence of malice, vengeance, thievery and duplicity, the darkness of the world became so pronounced that I felt like I was in Harlem in the middle of a gang fight. It was so thick, that it lay upon me like a summer's day when the heat and humidity are so high you can hardly breath and moving about feels almost impossible. Still it continued to grow until I became greatly encumbered by it. It weighed me down, my soul and spirit became greatly vexed and burden until I thought I would die under the weight of this suffocating evil. I could in no way touch my Savior! This world I was feeling, was so fearful and hazardous, that I felt desperate.

Suddenly, the Lord again began to emanate His holiness and purity, that terrible, wonderful holiness. The glow of His holiness was such brilliant a light; His whole being became filled with this awesome light. I began to discern His justice and mercy, His love and kindness. I began to again feel His gentleness and care as it surrounded me. Finally His majesty, that which strikes terror in the hearts of created beings. Then a wonderful peace began to encompass me as His splendor began to fill every inch of the air around me and every fiber of my being. His longsuffering love permeated every part of me until I began to rise up to meet Him in the air. Joy was effervescent as I continued to slowly rise up to Him. I wanted only to be with Him. I loathed the world, He was all I wanted and needed. How I wanted to be free of the world, so as I began to rise I did nothing to fight it, I was ready to go home. I was possessed with a divine love for Him such as I have known little of, and this love was enrapturing me.

Then Jesus broke into my happy state saying: *"Not yet, it's not yet time!"* Then I began to come back down to my bed. Jesus left, and I lay there in silence and awe at what had just happened.

We must make a choice; we can't have both, it is Jesus or the world!

——— ✦ ———

7/92 A WORD

"A WORD OF WISDOM"

"Don't set your eyes on things, not clothes, shoes or any other temporal thing, as they pull your eyes off Me. Do not concern yourself with any earthly

thing as they cannot satisfy, and they distract your passions from the One who alone can satisfy. Above all things keep your eyes wholly set upon Me, and reserve all your passions for Me for I alone can meet the deep needs of man." (Col. 3:1-3 Ephs.4:13)

———— ✦ ————

7/92 A WORD

"A WORD OF WISDOM"

I was in bed suffering as I had just fallen down a large flight of stairs, and hurt myself quite badly. I was unable to even walk to the next room without a tremendous amount of pain. I was walking across the room to go to the ladies room, when I asked the Lord saying: "Lord, what is the lesson you are wanting me to learn. I am in so much pain. If I only knew why You continue to allow such injury of my back, I would learn the lesson and be glad." Jesus then spoke audibly to me: *"To teach you submission in affliction."* I thought to myself, I thought I already understood that. I must not though or Jesus wouldn't still be trying to teach me this lesson. Well, I said to the Lord, I can barely walk, so I can't think of a better time to do an extensive study on the subject to see what I am missing. I did do this study and learned a great deal, which I put into practice resulting in a much deeper walk with the Lord! (Job 36:21, Heb.12, I Peter 4:12-14)

———— ✦ ————

"JESUS THE LAMB"

I was in prayer when I suddenly saw Jesus in an open vision standing in a beautiful meadow, surrounded by rolling hills. The meadow was filled with flowers, not a meadow like I have seen upon the earth, but one like I later saw in heaven. It was quiet and so peaceful.

Jesus became transparent and a large, fully-grown sheep appeared inside of Him. He continued to disappear until all that remained was the mature sheep. The Sheep who was Jesus then turned and walked on into the wilderness. Then the Holy Spirit spoke to my heart saying: *"I am going to give you the nature of the Lamb, so now be at peace!"* That was quite something as I knew instinctively that this would be given through hardships. Looking back, I was right. And His nature is still growing inside me.

"THE FIVE STAR GENERAL"

The Lord at times will instruct me of His ways through dreams and visions. As Jesus grants word pictures by this means, it is wonderful how it then becomes a beautiful revelation as it comes alive in His Word. In this dream, a man named Dale is the central character. Through it we will learn how the Lord makes His Five Star Generals.

Dale seemed to be one of a group of young people who lived on the streets in gangs, therefore he was pretty street-wise, rough and tough. They were the very epitome of carnality. None knew the other prior to their entrance into the kingdom. However because of their backgrounds, they had an immediate mutual affinity. Their antagonism toward authority was still at a height so they had a very difficult time relating to

Jesus. To further aggravate the situation, the passions of their flesh were pretty inflamed, so they tended to incite one another toward sin.

Jesus had a special purpose for Dale, so wisdom dictated that Dale be separated from his new friends, which was carried out with quickness and severity. This new state of things would remain until the Lord's purpose for them was solidified, and they were all far more stable in the faith, and not so given to the fancy of their flesh. To insure that they would continue in development and not turn back, He sharply reproved them for their failure. In fact, it seemed that many of our Lord's initial dealings with Dale especially, were hard, sharp and strong disciplines and chastisements. However, Jesus also demonstrated His strong love for Dale by the tender and gentle nurturing of his heart. Regardless of what occurred at any one time, the Lord's love and care for Dale remained full, rich and strong. His heart was always full of joyful expectation of Dale's ultimate victory. This hope never wavered regardless of how He might deal with him. Even the smallest victories were cause for immense joy and gladness in our Lord's heart. Again, Jesus never wavered in His hope or certainty that Dale would fulfill all that He had planned for him. He knew from the beginning that Dale would become a man of character, a man of strong, active, and noble faith and personality.

He would be capable of bearing much responsibility in meekness in his maturity, so Jesus knew what he was doing with him, and for what purpose He was preparing Dale. He would someday bear the responsibility of a Five Star General and would be one of the top leaders in Christ's Kingdom.

Yet in the beginning, the Lord's dealings with Dale had to be tough to break the rebellion. For this reason, His hand would stay pretty heavy upon him, and Dale would learn to trust and appreciate the fact that disciplines and chastisements were made a way of life for him. Jesus being the tenderhearted Shepherd that He is, and knowing the frailty of our human nature as He does, would not make Dale's path so tough without including along the way, the encouragements and praise as only the Lord could do. Albeit, the encouragements rarely seemed enough in Dale's eyes. Jesus would comfort him when he really needed it, but again, His comforts seemed to Dale, too little to match what Dale judged his need to be. Jesus would look upon Dale with great compassion when He saw him hurting, but He couldn't risk slowing down the pace of His work, as Dale had an appointment with destiny. When Dale really needed Jesus, I saw that Jesus was always there. But, our Lord would never do for Dale what he could do for himself.

On the other hand, every battle, every task was specially picked. The Lord would give Dale tasks and assign battles for him that were impossible to do without His divine help. The purpose for this was to force Dale's dependency upon Him, thereby breaking his self-sufficiency. The many times that Dale would sit down and whine, or want to quit saying that Jesus was too hard on him, or didn't care about him, Jesus would give Dale a little comfort and encouragement, and subsequently stir up situations to force him once again to the activity of moving forward in God's plan. (Prov. 3:11&12; 6:23 Amp.)

Dale's maturity was a project, which took many years to bring to perfection. But, by the time Jesus had accomplished it, His Kingdom had grown so large that it seemed to fill half the earth leaving room for only one other kingdom which was very evil.

As I looked around, everyone seemed quite busy. People were dressed in business suits, high-ranking military garb, and various medical uniforms as well as many other sundry professions and positions. I saw men and women of such nobility, each highly qualified for their task. All were people of stout character. Jesus had trained them all. Each were now fully equipped for their task.

Finally, the day of coronation had arrived. Dale had by then moved through the many levels of responsibility having fully embraced the tough ways of discipline by the Lord, and learned the lessons of the Kingdom well. He was now ready. He carried himself like a man of honor and cared only about the Kingdom business. His flesh had absolutely no hold on him whatsoever. He had been trained like a prince. (Proverbs 11:2&3 Amp.)

As was the Lord's custom for such an occasion, He had called the whole kingdom together to attend Dale's coronation. On the way to the amphitheater, I happen to overhear two men talking. One said to the other: "I wonder who it is this time?" The second man responded: "I don't know it might be Dale. Jesus has really been hard on him lately. That seems to be our Lord's way when He is nearing the completion of the preparation process." The second man then replied: "I am sure he must be of very high rank, as that is the only reason that He is ever so tough on someone." As we approached the sanctuary, the first man stated: "Yep, its Dale! I am so happy for him, as it has really been tough for him."

Once every one sat down, the orchestra began to play, "Crown Him with Many Crowns", during which Dale was escorted to the platform by a royal parade. As he stood before the whole assembly, he looked so regal. He held himself with such command, such dignity. Yet he was also a man of profound meekness.

A robe that looked like a king's robe was brought and laid upon his shoulders. As this was done, the robe became a military cape complete with medals of honor that had been earned in his many battles. His vestment was austere but bullet proof and was utterly impenetrable. Jesus then put a crown upon Dale's head as the orchestra once again played, "Crown Him with Many Crowns." However, this time the whole kingdom joined in. Dale was indeed crowned with a different crown for each of his major victories as depicted in Revelation 2 and 3. Following this a ring of king's authority was given him, and was put upon his finger. As he was crowned with the last crown, it became a military hat. As the scepter of iron was placed in Dale's hand, it became a scepter of gold in the shape of a cross. Having fully submitted to the scepter of iron; he was now qualified to reign with a scepter of gold, which depicted the authority of a crucified life. This authority is the highest authority given on earth, and only to those who have been fully crucified as Dale was.

As this phase of the ceremony came to an end, the whole kingdom gave him a standing ovation. Jesus waved His hand out toward the audience as though presenting Dale to them. He then turned to Dale and commended him saying: *"I am so pleased with you. This has been a day for which I have eagerly awaited from the beginning. Dale, the whole kingdom has been cheering you on all along the path. But, that had to stay hidden during the training. Now,"* Jesus continued: *"that you are here and receiving your commendations for which you have all this time been being prepared, you may now see the joy of the whole kingdom on your behalf."*

Because the work inside Dale had been so complete, the accolades meant nothing to him. His only desire was to righteously fulfill the trust now being bestowed on him. His will was set only to perform wisely and nobly all he was commissioned to do on behalf of the kingdom. Being circumspect in the handling of responsibility was his top priority. Last and most important of all, he longed with all his heart and soul to honor the One Whom had just honored him. Like a most respectful servant, he would serve with singleness of vision and nobility of purpose. Incidentally, Dale's wife was now standing by him; a royal helpmate.

I can't tell you Dear Reader, the difference between the rebellious hood that Dale once was compared to the high nobility that now stood before the whole kingdom receiving his commendations. What he had become under the tutelage and firm-handed discipline of our Lord had proven Christ's wisdom impeccable. The dream came to an end, and I awoke.

——— ◆ ———

"THE DISCIPLINE OF A PROPHET"

I went out to dinner with some friends after having a great inner battle. I wanted to go with them because I had not seen them in a long time and it was a special invitation over the holidays. On the other hand I wanted desperately to stay home and be with the Lord. I couldn't understand why the Lord would not want me to go, so I determined that it must just be my selfish desire to be with my Savior, so I went to dinner.

When I returned, I wished that I had not gone, for I really wanted to be with Jesus and by now I was feeling quite bad over having gone. So, I decided to spend a few hours in the Word and prayer. As I entered into prayer, I told the Lord: "Jesus, I long to be separated unto You alone. You are all I want!"

His immediate reply was: *"Why then can a prophet go out and make merry when My hand is heavy upon her to sit alone and weep."* I repented!

——— ✦ ———

1/93 A WORD

"A WORD OF WISDOM."

The Lord awakened me in the middle of the night and spoke thus to me: *"There is an element of bitterness in every task."*

——— ✦ ———

1/93 A WORD

"A WORD OF WISDOM."

Again, the Lord awakened me in the middle of the night and spoke thus to me. *"Nita clothe yourself with humility."* He followed that instruction by giving me (Col. 3:10,12-14). Please, understand that I have been steadily praying since the beginning of my salvation for humility. The Lord has graciously answered that prayer all along the way. But, this commandment was to enter into a deeper and more profound humility.

"And have put on the new man, which is renewed in knowledge after the image of him that created him. Put on therefore, as the elect of God, holy and beloved, bowels of mercies, kindness, humbleness of mind, meekness, longsuffering; Forbearing one another and forgiving one another, if any man have a quarrel against any: even as Christ forgave you, so also do ye. And above all these things put on charity, which is the bond of perfectness." Col. 3:10-14 K.J.

———— ◆ ————

2/93 A VISION

"WORD OF COMFORT AND WISDOM"

I was feeling a great deal of concern for a friend who was traveling through a season of suffering. Knowing this, in the middle of the night the Lord gave me a vision.

I saw a single, long, thin, white candle set in a silver candleholder. The candle was lit and sitting on a low table in the corner of my room. Lying at the foot of the candle was an open Bible. The corner was dark except the dim light given off by the candle, and a shaft of soft light that was beaming in through the window. The whole picture radiated peace, making it a welcome sight. This shaft of soft light beamed down upon the Bible and candle, as though illuminating and revealing its message of peace in the dark.

Suddenly a very thin beam of crisp, bright light shot up from the Bible into the air in an arch, then down into my heart. The words "tell (B), the key is forgiveness" entered my heart as the beam entered. The song "Holiness to the Lord" then began to play in my spirit, which lasted throughout the night. Although this was a message for my dear friend, it is also a message for all of us when we are going through affliction. *"Be quick to forgive." (Ephesians 4:32)*

—— ✦ ——

2/93 A DREAMS

"PROPHETIC DREAMS"

First Dream: I saw several couples sitting around a picnic table which was situated in the back yard of one of the couples. Some were ministers, some were not; some were non-Christians. They were all friends and were siting around laughing and drinking and behaving like the partygoers of the world. As I watched them party, I knew the secret sins of each one. I realized that some who were born-again were actually involved in adulterous affairs. The whole scene depicted their spiritual lives and spoke of a proverbial sin-entrenched lifestyle. Each, living lives filled with every kind of wickedness. Truly, one could not have recognized among them a Christian from an unbeliever. The dream ended and I awoke.

Second Dream: A man was standing on the bottom floor of what appeared to be an office complex awaiting the elevator on his floor. In front of Him were three elevator doors. He had been called up to receive his commission as captain, which was the highest possible promotion. As he stood awaiting the elevator, he suddenly noticed a fourth elevator door that had just appeared. This particular elevator had only two outlets however, one on the top floor and one on the bottom.

He then said as though it was a sudden revelation: "Oh this is the door that goes to the captains lounge at the top floor. That is the meeting place where the promotions are given. These three doors are for general traffic and do not go to the top floor. The fourth elevator, which I had not seen before, is for officers only. I guess the reason I had not seen it before was because I didn't need it before this." With that he stepped into the elevator to go to the top to get his commission.

Upon awakening, I received a vision of only one word. "Notwithstanding" A voice spoke this word to me simultaneously.

Third Dream: I was moving food around on what looked like grocer shelves, when suddenly the scene changed. Having by now been made a Captain I found myself walking into a huge, approximately 800 square foot executive office. I walked across the floor, and sat down in front of the executive's desk. The officer was a tall, slender, red-haired woman who was both well dressed and well groomed for her position. She was talking on the phone when I quietly sat down in front of her desk.

As I sat down, having ended her conversation, she put the phone back on the receiver. Then she pulled out a long-nosed revolver and pointed it over my right shoulder, as though she was going to shoot the gun.

I watched her closely, then said: "You know, He (God) isn't going to judge between the precious and the vile first. He is going to judge between the impure and the pure. The look of fear swept over her face, then putting the gun away, she replied as though just realizing it: "but He will temper the second group first." I responded: "That is right, that's right! Then His judgment will fall upon those who are doing their own thing, and going their own way in the name of the call; setting apart those who perform their call from the position of being on their knees before God."

So, all three dreams go together and speak to one another. If a man's lifestyle is like the first dream woe be unto him in this hour. God will first position His captains, then bring judgment upon those who qualify, as is indicated in the third dream. Once the Lord has judged the leaders He will then turn and wet His sword against those in His body who are living lives in gross sin.

The safest place for any minister to be who desires to fulfill his call, is on his knees before God. For any ministry not built on a foundation of prayer, will be brought down in this hour! (Col. 4:2 & I Thess. 5:17)

———— ✦ ————

"THE COMING PROPHETS"

While I was experiencing a kind of telescoping effect, zooming into the picture, the Lord spoke the following words. *"There are those of Mine who are so pure, so gentle, so lily white in their own eyes. They consider themselves the very righteous of My flock. There are these others whom I have specially picked; yet they run, they bolt, they chase back and forth!"*

On the second half of this statement the scene had effectively zoomed in on a prophet running down a crooked path literally bolting from one side of the path to the other. The scene depicted the skies to be dark and stormy. Each time this prophet would begin to stray to one side of the path or the other, a streak of lightening filled with the terror of the Lord would strike down on the path right at his feet, forcing him to turn in the other direction, thus correcting his straying.

The Lord continued: *"But in their chasing to and fro, in their bolting here and there; I guard them, I keep them, by the* **PROPHETIC ANOINTING!** (Great emphasis was l placed on the words in bold.)

This was seen in the lightening that struck the path of the prophet. Again, this scene was playing out as the Lord spoke in a voice that sounded like a trumpet.

As the vision was coming to a close, I saw many prophets on the path, each experiencing the same interplay between them and the Lord. Then I began to feel the fear of the body of Christ over the coming of these mighty men of valor. This fear was overwhelming. So, I asked the Lord why the Church feared their coming. His response was immediate. *"They are government, and to the Church an unbearable yoke."*

I was to see the nature and personality of these coming prophets, they are like Esaus, rough, ragged, strong willed and determined. Yet, honest about things as they are, or at least the way they saw them. You would never need to wonder where you stood with this individual, as they were an up-front kind of person. But, when refined by the Spirit of the Lord, they were Elijahs or John the Baptists.

—— ✦ ——

4/93 A PARABLE

"A PROPHETIC PARABLE"

I was asleep when I was suddenly awakened and moved upon by the Holy Spirit and taken into a trance where I lived out a parable. The Anointing shot from my tailbone through my stomach. With it, the words: "Spring forth into living!" This came forth in an authoritative command. As the bolt of life was released, it became a bike upon which I was riding. I found myself literally peddling this bike, being compelled to do so by the Holy Spirit. I started peddling kind of slow at first, and built up speed as I moved along, so that in moments, I was speeding. There seemed to be an extreme urgency to get on the road. Then the Holy Spirit spoke to me saying: "Your words will bring forth the cycle of life I am about to ignite."

"They are created now [called into being by the prophetic word], and not long ago; and before today you have never heard of them, lest you should say, Behold, I knew them!" (Isaiah 48:7 Amplified Bible)

I went back to sleep after a while, but was then awakened by the angel. He was by my side to take me on a trip to reveal to me the future. He picked me up in his arms and carried me through the night until we reached our destination. Although I am not free to relate what I was shown, and told, I am free to share something that happened along the way.

While we were flying through the sky, he was as I mentioned earlier, carrying me in his arms. As we were flying, he kept changing, from his non-glorified state to his glorified state. This was most interesting to me, as all but one angel that has appeared to me in the past have come in their glorified state. But this angel was originally not in his glorified state. In fact, had I passed him on the street, I would never have believed that he was an angel. He had age lines in his face. He was about 5ft 10 inches tall, thin, with an olive complexion. He looked like he was in his mid-thirties. He wore his medium brown hair in a sort of layered looked or long shagg. In length, his hair was about to his shoulders. To me, he was not particularly handsome. If he had been a man I would have thought he might have been from Greek ancestry because of his features. I make that a point here because of what I am going to say about him later.

Although it was in the dead of winter, he was wearing white paps such as you might see in Jamaica and a camel colored tunic while we were in flight. When we arrived at our destination, his clothes changed, and he had on a long white gown. As interesting as that was, it isn't the most had on a long white gown. As interesting as that was, it isn't the most remarkable event that took place. As I mentioned earlier, he changed in his appearance several times going from his non-glorified state, to his glorified state. When he was in his glorified state, he was breathtakingly beautiful. He also seemed to grow in size. I don't know that he grew in height, as I would have had no way to measure that. But he did grow in size. He went from being thin and rather a small frame for a man, to looking like he was a weightlifter. He was extremely mussle-bound. Not in a way that was unattractive, just the opposite, he was superb looking. His hair shone with the glory of heaven and glistened in the light of the moon. I would not call him handsome, but perfect in beauty! I would say that in his glorious state, that he outshined the light of the moon, or the sun either one. His eyes became piercing with the glory, yet filled with love. He truly was a glorious being. In fact, he was no less glorious than most of the angels I have seen. There are those exceptions, because of the place of their abode with the Father. Those angels bear a glory and beauty that is far more extraordinary.

When he would talk to the Father, which, he did often, he would speak in his heavenly language, which I could not understand or begin to interpret. However, as he spoke my heart would always burn within me. (Luke 24:32) It seemed as though the Holy Spirit was monitoring all that he said and did, as he said and did nothing without first checking with the Lord. He wouldn't answer even one of my questions without first asking the Lord. It would be during these times of communication with the Lord that he would change into his glorified state becoming so beautiful and holy. It would always take my breath away for just a moment when this change would occur.

I asked the Lord why He was allowing me to see this. He spoke immediately: *"There is one glory on earth, and another in heaven."* (I Corinthians 15:40-43 K.J.) I was immediately given to know that just as I saw this angel's body transformed into this glorified state, our bodies would be equally transformed into a glorified state. No matter, how unattractive we feel we are on earth, we will be utterly glorious in appearance in heaven. In fact, it is in this glorified state that God sees us through the blood even now!

—— ✦ ——

4/93 A WORD

"PROPHETIC WORD"

I received a prophetic word in prayer. "Separator—coming through once again in a much elevated way. Some to move, some to stay, some to rise up in the fray. Can we stand? Can we endure the day of His coming? Awake, awake oh Zion! For the sword is swiftly coming. Those who sowed in tears, will reap in joy. Those who sowed in vanity shall reap in tears. Nevertheless He comes to purge the temple as a refiner's fire, the sons of Levi."

"Bow before Him, love and adore Him. Remove the hindrances that separate you from Him. In the great Citadel hide. For who in the temple court will stand in the day of His coming. Weep and lament for the unfaithful priest is brought low, and the voice of the prophet will be resounding once again. O, but how we fear the day of their coming. Mighty and terrible will they be in the day of their lifting up. Eyes, flames of fire, with a sword in their hand to wreak vengeance on the enemy, and to deliver the poor in the land. Arise now, blow the trumpet, for Jehovah is coming—He comes, He comes!"

———— ✦ ————

3/93 A VISISON

"THREE TREES"

I saw three trees, each one being distinct from the other. These distinctions revealed the degree of separation of the trees unto the Father.

The first tree was beautiful and was clothed in the glory of the Lord. The second tree was even more beautiful and was clothed in a much greater glory, its fruit was healthy and delectable to the pallet. For this reason it was far more majestic in appearance. The beauty of the third tree was even more magnificent than the other two by far. Its fruit was plentiful, exceeding large in size, and was of the most excellent flavor. It was clothed in a far more majestic glory. It shone with such radiance and brilliance that it utterly surpassed the other two and could in no way be compared to the other two.

A voice spoke to me from heaven and explained that the first tree depicted most of His Church. They love the Lord and He loves them. But they spent little time with Him and continued on knowing no special separation unto the Father. For this reason, they are beautiful for they are His, but bear little glory as they spend so little time in His presence, requiring instead the company of other people. For this reason, its limits in fellowship of His glory are forever sealed.

The second tree is far more beautiful, bearing far greater glory. The reason the second tree stands so, is that it knows a peculiar separation unto God. This tree spends extended time in His presence, enjoying Him and bringing forth the fruit of their fellowship. Although this was true, the second tree still felt they needed the fellowship of other people as well. Therefore it was not willing to be fully separated unto the Lord. The Father greatly loves this second tree, and they love Him, however the degree of glory the second tree will bear and the fruit it will bring forth is forever sealed.

The third far excelled the other two in glory. The reason for the extraordinary difference is that this tree has dedicated its life in total separation unto God, and requires His fellowship alone. For this reason the Father has not put a ceiling upon the glory it shall bear, nor the fruit it will bring forth. It is most pleasing to Him and will ever bring Him much glory, joining in the fellowship of both His suffering and His glory. And in both seasons with the husbandman, it shall bring forth extraordinary fruit, much to the Father's great pleasure. Finally, this tree is cocooned in a special presence and protection of the Father that only this third tree shall ever know.

—— ✦ ——

7/93 A VISITATION

"A STOP IN PARADISE"

Today I was pouring out my heart to the Lord. I was telling Him how much I loved and missed Him. For in order to more fully purge me and develop my faith, I have been in a wilderness and without the manifested presence of my Savior for a long time.

Suddenly, the spirit world was opened up to me. I became wrapped in the Lord's presence, then my spirit began to ascend to my Father. I was at first taken to paradise where I saw majestic mountains. These mountains had colors and hues that seemed to me to be living, and were far more beautiful than anything I had ever seen on earth. Some of the highest peaks seemed to have snow on them. So, they appeared to be snow-capped. But I later discovered that it is the way God's glory sits upon these higher peaks that cause them to look snow-capped. I also saw the tree covered foothills, which in themselves were also very beautiful. I saw lush valleys, and lovely verdant meadows wonderfully sprinkled with a fragrant and colorful array of wilderness flowers. I saw broad streams and a mountain lake with crystalline blue water. The whole sight was unbelievably beautiful and restful. My Granddaughter who has been taken to heaven several times as well, is quite familiar with this place as she has been there a few times with Jesus.

The sky was crisp and blue, it was a picture of the most supreme tranquility. Then I began to ascend again. Up I went and right into the Father's arms. My head resting upon His bosom. I felt Him put His arms around me, and a deep rest and peace began to fill me. I felt so loved, so protected, I was with the One for Whom my soul greatly longed. I was appreciative of the fact that He had allowed me to see another part of paradise that I had never seen before, but for now I was in the lofty arms of my Father for whom my soul was longing. The wilderness is beautiful, but it is God who satisfied my longing.

———— ✦ ————

"A CLOUD OF REVELATION"

Shortly after midnight, I awoke. I knew I was not going to get back to sleep, so I began to meditate upon the deeper life in Christ. I was then wrapped in a cloud of revelation. The revelation the Father was giving began to permeate my entire being.

"Fellowship with the Father, in its deepest and truest sense is beyond reason. Although a certain essence of understanding can filter down through the system of the mind, the highest essence of this fellowship cannot be comprehended but by the spirit. The upward spiral of this holy fellowship will ultimately incorporate the mind, the heart, the soul, and the will, at last bringing even the flesh to rest in God. This is so that the whole faculty of man be emerged in the quest for God. All the seeker's being, zealously seeking his Lord while at rest in the Supreme.

God conveys Himself through our spirit, our spirit thus relating the intelligible understanding to our minds and hearts. The Holy Spirit working silently in our will causing us to desire His supreme will. (Romans. 8:16 and Phil. 2:13) He continues to work giving our mind knowledge, our hearts understanding, filling us with wisdom and holiness until we are transfigured into His image. The final stages of this transaction are the crucifixion of the sin nature and union with Christ. This union, is then sealed with the impartation of the government of righteousness." (I Corinthians. 2:10-16; 2 Corinthians. 3:18, 4:11 & 12; Romans 12:2)

Being by now so permeated with His Spirit, I was lifted into the quiet and rest of His love so completely that I became enlarged with the realization that man was made for Him alone. This, I quietly spoke to Him. Further, only when all our faculties are at rest in Him being fully emerged in Him, can we be complete. Only when all our faculties find their center in Christ, can we know, and be at rest and content with the purpose for life. There is no life outside of man's habitation in Christ. There is no purpose to be served in life outside of man's response to the all-encompassing call to enter into union with Christ Jesus. Abandoning ourselves to that call means experiencing the completion of ourselves for which we desperately yearn.

I was totally embraced in the full reality of these things, my innermost being so utterly saturated by the Lord Himself, that at last I felt utterly complete. All wandering had come to an end, and I was at rest in God! There I stayed for a good long while!

I shared this with you, as I want you to know, that all our searching is vanity and frivolousness if it is not a solitary seeking for Christ alone. We must seek first the Kingdom of God, and His righteousness, then all these things will be added unto you.

--- ✦ ---

12/93 A VISITATION

"A VISITATION"

What began as a vision unfolded into a visitation. I was walking down a long path teaching on the things of the Kingdom and the ways of God, when a friend came to join me. I began to share with him the treasures of the Kingdom. Then Jesus came to me and told me the following: "All that we do, except those things which flow from the Spirit of Christ, are sin. This includes even the most righteous of our deeds".(Isaiah 64:6) The idea was that 100% of our Christian acts are stained with sin because of the presence of the sin nature in our soul. "This remains true," He said: "until the sinful nature is crucified and Christ has come to live in our souls, thereby living His life out through us." Jesus then spoke some other things to me, and while we were talking I watched my sin be removed from me like a murky film and fall upon Jesus about every five minutes or so. Then, His righteousness would leave Him through His hands and fall upon me like a clean white spiritual blanket. This occurred several times. Each time that it happened, Jesus would smile, as He would be so delighted to take my sin upon Himself.

Then Jesus said: "This is the way it happens. Your sin is ever being imputed to Me and My righteousness to you!"

Then changing the subject Jesus said: "Don't be concerned when people reject you Nita for speaking to them about their sin and telling them about the demands of the Father. People do not like their self-righteousness being tampered with. They want to remain comfortable in it and left alone, but, if they really want truth, though they initially fight it, they will be back.." Then He left!

--- ✦ ---

"A WORD OF WISDOM"

The Lord spoke to me in a dream about the vision that He puts in the hearts of His own. He said: *"The vision needs to go deep; deep enough that it becomes a means of purging to the soul."* (Ps 105:19) *"It needs to be humble; humble enough to break the pride and self-seeking of the vessel. It must bear simplicity; that is singleness and sincerity. It must require wisdom; a wisdom that demands and establishes the vessel in total dependence upon God."*

—— ✦ ——

1/94 A VISION

"JESUS ON THE CROSS"

I looked and saw the heavens open. It was as though someone had cut them open with a surgical knife revealing what was within. As this occurred, what was exposed was the glory of God. Oh, it was utterly beautiful. This incision looked as though it was filled with liquid light, brilliant, radiant light, undefiled and pure!

I gazed at this heavenly sight with wonder. After a short time, I began to feel that I was missing something. So, I began to search as deeply into the incision as I possibly could, straining to see what it was that I was missing. I would blink and try to look harder; and would find that each time I would do this, the glory would increase in brightness. I continued feeling this need to look deeper until I could find what it was that I was missing. Consequently, I broadened my search, when I realized that the invisible surgical knife had sliced more than a vertical line in the heavens. It had also cut a horizontal line near the top of the vertical, making in the heavens, a Cross of light. It was a radiant and glorious Cross of glory.

Instinctively, I knew there was yet more to be seen. So, I continued my search, probing ever deeper into the Cross of light. Again, as I did this, the intensity of glory would continue to grow brighter, the light each time becoming many times greater than before. Because of the increase of glory, it was becoming increasingly difficult to look into the light, but I so wanted to see what it was that God had for me. So, I continued to peer deeply, evermore deeply into the Cross of Light. Then finally I saw it. It was the Cross. It was the Lord's Cross! Yet, it was not an old brown Cross full of splinters. It was a Cross of a pure and slightly transparent gold light. Again, it is so difficult to express the inexpressible beauty of the glorious things. But, beautiful beyond words it was. This Cross was radiant with the glory of the Lord.

I blinked my eyes again for just a moment. Then I returned my attention to the heavens. When I did, I saw hanging on the Cross, my Savior! He too was radiant with this same golden glow. Yet, He was upon the Cross in all its horror and suffering. I saw His wonderful being repeatedly convulse with pain as He hung there. Yet, the love and the glory that emanated from Him amidst His anguish was so compelling. I wept in the deepest love and gratitude to Him. Still the glory continued to increase in its radiance and splendor.

At last the Father's voice broke through the painful scene in front of me saying: *"He did this for you!"* When He spoke this to me, His words filled every part of my being, and I wept as I have never wept before. I wept so hard as I had never known, with such a loving gratitude, to my wonderful Savior for what He had done for me.

How cherished we are by our Father in heaven, that He would permit His Son to pay such a price for us. The wonder of the love of the Son for us, that He would be not only willing, but oh so desirous to suffer such atrocities for the sake of mankind. His love compelled Him to give what no man could ever have done. He gave His life for us, how grateful we should be for all that our wonderful and gentle Savior has done.

—— ✦ ——

"THE ROBE OF RIGHTEOUSNESS"

In prayer today, the Lord quickened (2 Cor. 5:4 K.J.) to me. *"For we that are in this tabernacle do groan, being burdened: not for that we would be unclothed, but clothed upon, that mortality might be swallowed up of life."* Jesus then imparted the whole scripture upon the tablet of my heart, and I fell into deep travail.

I then saw a vision. I saw the garment of righteousness descending from heaven coming down to clothe my naked soul. It was so beautiful. It was a garment of light, whiter than any white on earth. It was translucent with the glory of the Lord, in fact, it was the glory of the Lord. It was actually a very part of God Himself.

So, I was instructed that we groan under the burden of our nakedness, yearning to be clothed over, but not with this tent of flesh. Nor do we necessarily want to be free of this mortal body, as we need it to travel through our pilgrimage on this earth. Notwithstanding, we long to be further clothed over with our heavenly body. This is a temple not made with hands but by the living God, and a temple that fits over our soul in beautiful splendor. It is being clothed with Christ!

"But put ye on the Lord Jesus Christ, and make not provision for the flesh, to fulfill the lusts thereof." (Romans. 13:14 K.J.)

———— ◆ ————

12/93 A WORD

"WORD OF WISDOM"

The Lord spoke to me in a vision saying: "In revival, the cloud of fear is removed from the mind, heart and soul. Then the mind, heart and soul are filled with faith. So, pray for revival, not only for the reviving of the saints, but for the preservation of My Church in a time of persecution."

———— ◆ ————

5/94

"A VISION"

The Lord spoke to me in a vision saying: *"The flesh of man is hindering the purity of the Gospel."* I saw in this vision that the flesh of man was causing the Gospel to appear to be something it is not. I also saw how this impure Gospel is adversely affecting both the Church and the unbeliever. I then experienced the grieving of the Holy Spirit over this reality. But, not without the promise that God is going to undertake and bring forth the pure, healing the Church and redeeming the willing unbeliever.

———— ✦ ————

5/94 A VISITATION

"JESUS WEEPS FOR HIS CHURCH"

I had just finished ministering a message, which called the Church to which I was ministering into holiness. It was obvious to me that there was resistance to the message. It wasn't something a person could see with their eyes. But, I could feel it in the spirit.

So, when I finished ministering the Word, instead of moving back in to worship right away. I decided to pray for the Church. The Church universal, and the immediate Church in front of me was the object of my prayers. When suddenly Jesus appeared in front of me. I could see the Church, that is His body through His eyes. As He stood on the platform, I saw tears of compassion and grief flowing down His bronze cheeks as He spoke to His body.

"You have ears with which to hear, but you do not hear. You have eyes to see, but you do not see. You have a heart with which to understand, but you do not understand. I have spoken to you about the beautiful things of the kingdom, I have unveiled to you lovely things of My Father and your Father, yet you cannot see and you do not hear. I told you how the meek would inherit the earth, how the merciful would obtain mercy. I said to you blessed are the poor, for theirs is the Kingdom of Heaven. I shared with you how the pure in

heart shall see God, and many such things have I spoken to you, but you would not hear. Therefore the day is coming when you shall lose what I have offered. The day of visitation will be over, and you will suffer the loss. So, now My people, wake ye up and hear before every door of the precious things be shut up to you and another takes the gold that was offered to you."

It caused Him great pain to speak this way to His people.

I shared with the local Church everything that Jesus had spoken. Rather than anger, they surprisingly opened their hearts, and the anointing of the Holy Spirit came into the Church in such a way that I could hardly stand for the glory and sweetness of communion the people were sharing with their Lord. Even so, all that Jesus said would happen did occur in the sight of two years. Much pain and sorrow came to that body from which they never did recover. Just as His Word was fulfilled there my Dear Reader, it will be fulfilled throughout His Church, unless we humble ourselves and open our heart to His correction and teachings of the cross.

—— ✦ ——

6/94 A VISITATION

"DIVINE LOVE"

I was on my daily walk with a friend, when a voice spoke to me saying: *"Would you be willing to take someone's cancer so I could heal them?"* I immediately replied: "I rebuke you Satan." So, my friend asked: "what did you see?" I answered her: "Nothing, its all right." We walked a little way further, and again, this voice asked me if I would be willing to take someone's cancer so that He could heal them. Again, I came against Satan, but this time I added: "I don't need to take anyone's cancer so they can be healed, Jesus did that on the Cross 2000 years ago." Again Bonnie asked me what was going on, so I explained to her what had happened. But, the thoughts of it weighed heavily upon me. I couldn't let go, wondering if in fact it could be the Lord.

When I returned home, I received a call saying that a dear friend had cancer. I was aghast! They wanted to know what the Lord was saying, would they live? I hung up the phone and asked the Lord what was going on. I no sooner got those words out and the phone rang again. Another friend reaching out, they have cancer. What is the Lord saying, will she live? Well I didn't know the answer to either one of their questions. First, I had to have the answer to my own question.

So, I prayed. I said: "Lord that was You in the park wasn't it? I don't understand, why would you ask me to do something that Jesus did 2000 years ago?" My Lord was silent. I said: "Lord, what are you saying to me, won't You please speak to me?" Then He questioned: *"Will you take your friend's cancer so I can heal her?"* I knew to which friend He was referring. I started thinking about her family; their need for her, their love for her, and how devastating it would be for the family to lose their mom. I also thought about the fact that if I did take this cancer, I would not die, but live perhaps years as I have seen others do with horrific pain. I would be required to answer the call that was on my life, and still I would not die to escape the pain, I would live until I died as a martyr, as that is how I had already been told I would die. I thought about my own daughter and the pain she would go through watching me suffer in this way. Then I thought about my friend's family once again. How can I choose me over her? Well, I couldn't! So, with my eyes filled with tears, I told the Lord, yes, I would be willing to take her cancer, if He would heal her. Immediately the Lord replied to me: *"Will you take the cancer of the other, so that I can heal her?* I smarted under that question. "Lord," I responded: "This lady, I have sought to be a friend as well, you know that. But, she has chosen to make herself my enemy. Every time I am alone with her, she sends darts into my heart.

She has never been willing to open her heart to me; but, purposefully has determined to be my enemy." Again, the Lord asked me: *"Nita, will you take her cancer, that I might heal her?"* I thought and thought. I thought again about all the pain, from which, I could not so much as hope for death to escape my agony. Why such a fatalistic view? That is what was placed in my heart. I knew that if I said yes, it would mean entering into the depths of suffering with cancer, so that these others could go free. I also knew that God doesn't play games, if He is asking me to do this, I need to respond to him fully expecting to receive this cancer, that these ladies might be healed. I felt so much love and compassion for both mothers, their children and their husbands. How could I choose myself over them, not even for Ricci, my daughter's sake. I mean, why should my daughter be spared this grief when the children of these mothers would have to bear their grief if I said no to the Lord. It was a very difficult decision to make, only because I knew it was no game! Finally, after about 10 minutes, I answered my Savior! "Jesus, I will take their cancer. I will take the cancer of both women if you will heal them."

Immediately and unexpectedly, heaven opened, a waterfall of the love of God began to pour down upon me and into my whole being. This love was nothing like I had ever experienced before. It was filled with compassion, care, mercy, thoughtfulness, tenderness, and the longing for the good of the object of its affections. The desire for the well being of the person was so great and all encompassing that the sacrifice of His own well being to meet the need of the object of His affection would not require even so much as a second thought. Such sacrifice was second nature to my Lord. I could feel very clearly that this was true of both friends and of His enemies. There was absolutely no difference in His own heart. One deserved the same love and care as the other without thought of the price He might pay to fulfill love's requirement. As this love flowed down over me in waves, I wept and wept. Then He said: *"Nita, today, you have touched divine love."* I knew Jesus was saying that I had entered, in a small way to the love with which He loves all mankind, whether, a person is a Satan worshipper, an all around good hearted person who has never been saved, or the most mature Christian. In some small measure I had learned a little more about His heart.

My friends, I wept, and I wept with joy, thankfulness and love for Jesus and for all people, for a good long time. When I later rose up, I did so fully expecting to wake up some time soon with the effects of cancer.

I discovered within a couple days that one of the ladies had apparently been healed. So, I waited quietly and patiently for the cancer. Another couple days went by. The Lord then awakened me at midnight from a sound sleep. He told me with love pouring over me: *"I will always protect you from getting cancer because you were willing to lay down your life for your enemy."* The fear that I had lived with since a young child that I would someday get cancer was immediately gone. He shared with me that I had been tried as Abraham was tried regarding Isaac, and that He was very pleased with my response.

—— ✦ ——

7/94 A REVELATION

"SEPARATION UNTO GOD."

Today in prayer, the Lord first showed me how literally unworthy our souls were to be the dwelling place of God and to be further clothed with God. Our souls are so utterly defiled. I then saw in our birth as newborn babies; aside from the sin nature that abides in us all, our souls are pure and innocent. I then saw how I had spent my whole life defiling it with self-government, self-sufficiency, self-will, carnal lusts and pride. All these and much more make the soul unworthy of Him. Yet, Jesus desires it for His dwelling place. So, upon salvation, the Holy Spirit goes to work preparing the soul to be the Lord's habitation, for He desires the soul as much as He desires the spirit. He sets Himself to bring us to desire the freedom, then begins the work to free us from the reign of the sinful nature, and the unholy wounds and stain of sin. The Holy Spirit continues restoring the willing soul until He has purged it of all, including the sinful nature. Then Jesus comes into our now purified soul, to at long last dwell and be at rest. As the Lord brought me to this conclusion, I felt a sort of cylindrical spiritual wall come down directly from the Father, and completely surround my soul. The world and the spirit of the world were totally severed from me. I was at last totally set apart unto God.

There was immediately such a uniting of my soul to God, that He was all I could feel, sense and experience. The spiritual cylinder that covered me kept me protected from all that is depictive of the world. Thus enabling me to draw directly from Him as my source, without interference. I felt so loved, so protected, so severed from the world, and owned by God alone. My soul was virtually encapsulated by a fortress of God Himself. Hence, His life was constantly flowing into me through this capsule. I was in a constant tangible communion, with the Father, the likes of which I had never before known. It was a most wonderful experience. It was difficult to have it come to an end as I would give anything to ever-live in that wonderful place with Him. I know when His work of preparation is complete, I will at last enjoy this most ardently sought holy union with my Lord forever. Come Lord Jesus, come!

——— ✦ ———

"A VISIT TO THE THRONE"

This morning while I was on my morning walk with my dear friend Bonnie, I began to share with her about (Ephesians 2:4 & 5 K.J.). *"But God, who is rich in mercy, for his great love wherewith He loved us, Even when we were dead in sins, hath quickened us together with Christ."* As I began to share this, my spirit was taken before the Throne of the Lord. As I stood before Him, He began to wash me with a liquid light, waves of brilliant, healing light full of wisdom. Over and over again, this light would wash over me like a waterfall of glory. What it immediately produced in my heart was an explosion of joy, which would burst through my heart repeatedly. With each new wave of glory washing down over me, a new explosion of joy would burst through my heart. It would be so intense in my body on earth, that I was not able to move for a moment.

Then the Lord began to expound to me regarding His purpose for creating all that He created. He began with: *"Nita, do you know why I created the heavens and the earth?"* I responded with: "I don't Lord." So, He continued: *"Nita, do you know why I created the sun, the moon, and the stars of the universe?"* I then replied with the only answer with which I could respond: "I don't know Lord." He continued: *"Do you know why I created the earth, in all its beauty?"* Again, I responded with: "No Lord."

He was leading me somewhere and I didn't know where, but I knew that whereever it was, I wanted to follow. Again the Lord questioned: *"Do you know why I created the great towering mountains, the beautiful valleys, the lakes and rivers, and the trees and shrubs of the field. Do you know why I created the flowers of such beauty, colorful and bearing every kind of pleasant fragrance, and the herbs of the field?"* I repeated: "No Lord, I do not."

"Do you know why I created the birds of the air and the fish of the sea, both small and great; and the beasts that roam the earth?" Again, I replied: "No Lord." *"I picked a place and there made a lovely garden, it was the most beautiful place in all the earth. A place of My special attention and care. Do you know why?"* I again said: "No, Lord."

He responded with such tenderness: *"I created all that I created, so that I could create man and give him a pleasant and beautiful place in which to dwell. Nita, do you know why I created man?"* Where the Lord was taking me with all His questions I still did not know. All I knew was that my heart was filled with love for Him, and my soul was filled with joy. So I followed.

He continued: "*I created man, knowing that the day would soon come that he would rebel against me, plunging the human race into sin and decay which would result in untold suffering. I knew before I laid the foundations of the earth that I would need to send My Son to redeem fallen humanity. Still, I elected to create man. Do, you know why?*" Again, I responded: "No, I don't Lord."

With this the Lord began to share His heart. He continued: "*Nita, I had one purpose in mind when I created all these things. My purpose was to create man. For thousands of years I have had but one desire. My heart has longed, as no human can understand, to see this desire fulfilled. So great was this yearning, that I sent my Son to die on Calvary, a ransom for many. I yearned with such longing to redeem man from his fallen state, that I might bring those who were willing back to Myself. Do you know why?*" "Lord, I do not know why," was again my response to His question: "*This desire,*" He continued: "*that I have carried in My heart all these years, out of My great mercy toward man was to draw him back to Myself to satisfy My great love for him. This was a love, which could only be fully satisfied in one way. I have waited and yearned from generation to generation for this very hour when at last My longing could be realized. And, Nita, you have never known a longing, until you have known the longing of your God.*" At that moment my heart was filled with His great longing. This, was a love so great, it was incomprehensible. His was a love that is filled with an unquenchable yearning for union with the soul of redeemed man.

He continued: "*That longing Nita, is that I could once again after so long a time indwell the soul of man and be vitally united to him as I was with My Son when He was on the earth. In this generation, I will have a people who will forsake all to overcome the world, their flesh and the devil in order to have union with Me, having My Son indwell their inner-most being. Then at last My yearning will be satisfied.*"

By this time I was exploding with joy, a joy that felt like it was exploding out of my innermost being. A joy that was coming out of the knowledge that our God, for Whom I have sought with such ardent zeal from the beginning of my Christian walk, truly wants me more than I could ever want Him. As great as my wanting continues to be, I still marvel with awesome delight and streaming tears of thankfulness every time I ponder this wonderful experience with My Lord. How much it means to Him to have this union with those who love Him. He is not content to simply indwell our spirits. He wants all of us.

When He had spoken all that He wanted me to hear, I was immediately back in body. (Ephesians 2:4; Titus 2:13 & 14)

———— ✦ ————

7/94 A REVELATION

"THE FEAR OF DEATH"

In prayer today, I experienced the revelation that the fear of death is actually the fear of being eternally separated from God. Then I experienced how Satan rules the heart of man through this fear, leading it into every conceivable vice. The fear of death creates the need for a god, whether it be the god of self, a god made by human hands, a god that has essentially evolved such as the worship of money ect., or a person. Once the true God has been removed from His rightful place in our hearts, man must find something or someone to take His place. Notwithstanding, it must be something that we subconsciously feel can pacify the anguish so deep in our hearts. An anguish that has been created through this haunting fear of death ~ man must have a god who will promise life in the eternal. If he doesn't outright offer this promise, the mind will somehow create it, or deny the existence of eternity. Yet the anguish will continue, for separation from God, resulting in eternal punishment is nevertheless real, and our deepest heart knows it. For the One Who was meant to be the Rock of salvation reigning in the soul, has been forced out, hence the soul feels the void, thus the anguish.

Through pride, and carnal lust we seek to pacify this grieving wound, or numb our senses to it, ignorant of the fact that Christ is the only Healer of this anguish. (Jeremiah 10:19) For some I suppose, the search continues leading them ever further from the True Source, for their hearts are bent on rebellion and will never return to the Rock Who offers their salvation in His blood. Whatever the case may be, these deceptive quests result in the destruction of the soul, eternally. (Hebrews. 2:15)

———— ✦ ————

8/94 A DREAM

"THE CHURCH OF REVELATION"

This is the state of the Church in the free world. The Church is an institution of rules, form, and tradition, but the true life as depicted in the book of James is missing. Thus, God looks at the Church and sees a perversion of the true. We are not a Church who is enlivened by the Spirit, as we are called to be. We fall miserably short. It is not God who rules the Church of the free world, it is the religious spirit, hence; this Church is a perverted replica of God's true Church.

The problem is a matter of the heart. We worship God, but our hearts are far from Him. Some give tithes and offerings, but hate their brother. Others serve with fervor, yet have little love in their hearts, or covet their neighbor's possessions, whether it is their wife, or their property. It is a heart issue.

Revelation 3:15 (K.J.) speaks of the Church of the free world. Let me share it with you.

"I know thy works, that thou art neither cold nor hot: I would that thou wast cold or hot. So then, because thou art lukewarm, and neither cold nor hot, I will spew thee out of my mouth. Because thou sayest, I am rich, and increased with goods, and have need of nothing; and knowest not that thou are wretched and miserable, and poor, and blind, and naked: I counsel thee to buy of me gold tried in the fire, that thou mayest be rich; and white raiment, that thou mayest be clothed, and that the shame of thy nakedness do not appear: and anoint thine eyes with eye salve, that thou mayest see. As many as I love, I rebuke and chasten: be zealous therefore, and repent. Behold, I stand at the door and knock: if any man hear my voice, and open the door, I will come in to him, and will sup with him, and he with me. To him that overcometh will I grant to sit with me in my throne, even as I also overcame, and am set down with my Father in His throne. He that hath an ear, let him hear what the Spirit saith to the churches.

Please don't put this book down now! Read on, for if you don't see it, I understand, as I didn't see it either until the Lord revealed it to me. So, read on and see if it will make sense to you in the end.

The standard of true religion is a matter of the heart. True religion frees us from the rule of the religious spirit who keeps us locked in a spiritual delusion. The Church in Laodicea was under a paralyzing delusion as well. They honestly did not know they were deluded. They apparently were not in any terrible sin, they simply did the works of God while clinging to the world, thus keeping themselves locked in the claws of a religious spirit. It is of this fiend that God desires to free His children today, to enable us to break through to the true power of God.

James gives the antidote for this delusion. He tells us that as a Christian we are to learn the ways of the self-sacrificing and divine love for all, showing no partiality. We are to keep ourselves free of the contamination and defilement of the world, reigning over sin in our own life. The authentic Christian bridles his tongue, and lives to fully obey the Word of God. He gives to the needs of the poor and needy, because he loves the poor as he would his own son. His heart toward an offender is one of mercy, regardless of the type or degree of the offense. This is true because the authentic Christian has learned Divine love for all, friend or foe. He is pure in heart, humble, compassionate, free of covetousness, and is wholly submitted to God. He, because of his great love for his neighbor is a true peacemaker, neither judging falsely, nor critical of another. He is a person of prayer, walking in the spirit and loving the Word of God. Finally, he is a person who has been inwrought with the power of meekness and humility, and is therefore patient in all situations, and with those who are weak and erring. He is the picture of Christ. Few knew Jesus as well as His brother James. They grew up together. James had seen Jesus in every kind of situation and conflict, and learned this was truly the way of God. It is out of the years of experience with Jesus as well as his own years of shepherding the flock of God and growth in Christ, that he writes. James was a man of fervent prayer. History tells us that when he died, it was discovered that his knees where callused like an elephants skin, from the many hours that he spent on his knees in prayer. It was through this very means that he eventually came to be so much like Christ himself.

This is what the Laodicean Church needed to do. They needed to do all that James stipulates in his Epistle. If they obeyed, they met the standards that Jesus was calling them to. This is where we stand today. We are like the Laodicean Church who thinks we can have the ways of the world that seem clean and innocent, and Jesus too. This has left us in a perversion of true religion, and a need for change. As we look at the things that Jesus is saying and we seek to make the changes that He desires, through much prayer, we will be exceedingly pleasing to Him. Living holy and God honoring lives will cause our worship to be holy in His eyes. It is our consecrated life that flows up to the Lord as a sweet odor, a precious sacrifice and wonderful fragrance to be deeply and lovingly appreciated by Him. In a consecrated life, all perversion is gone and holiness becomes the standard of excellence that can be blessed by Him.

—— ✦ ——

9/94 A VISION

"AMERICA AND THE EAGLE"

I saw myself in the midst of some other Christians whose faces kept changing. When these changes would occur, the whole person would become this other individual. In this way the Lord was depicting a large mass of people instead of a handful.

I began to look around and saw a flagpole upon which sat the American eagle in statue form. I watched it for a moment as I was strangely drawn to it. The eagle suddenly became alive and began to grow to an enormous size. This alteration in the eagle provoked my full attention as I continued to gaze upon it with intensity and anticipation. The eagle continued to grow until it became the size of a man with a tremendous wing span. By this time it was an incredibly majestic bird which struck awe in my heart. It then began to mount up off the top of the flagpole. As it began to lift of the top of the pole, the eagle continued to grow in size, until it was at least double the size of a man. Because of the eagle's immense size, all its movements seemed very animated, and deliberate. Every movement was like watching a living cinemascope unfold. As this by now enormous bird spiraled ever higher, he continued to grow and his every move was so animated that it took my breath away. I was in awe of his beauty and grandeur. As he circled around us, his circles continued to become larger until each circle was enormous in size. I then noticed that he had an olive branch in his mouth, and in his huge talons he carried a log. He continued to mount and continued to grow in size until he was the size of a large house.

I began to yell at people around me to look at the eagle, but I could not get anyone's attention. I yelled feverishly trying to get the attention of people, but no one would listen to me. I wanted them to see the eagle that had left the flagpole.

Finally, the eagle broke out of his mount, and began to fly off. As he did, he flew over a river, and dropped the log in the river. He then immediately disappeared. I was astonished, I didn't know what to do. The most significant thing in the history of America had just occurred, and I could get no one to listen to me. The Lord spoke to me when the eagle disappeared, saying; today, I have dropped the ball on America. My special covering has been removed, and you will soon see the effects of it.

——— ✦ ———

"THE ANGEL OF JUDGMENT"

I saw myself walking from city to city in America. My family was with me. As we entered into the particular city at dark, we saw a huge glorious angel driving a magnificent Roman style chariot, which was being pulled by an equally magnificent white, war-horse. Both were surrounded by a glorious heavenly light, which struck fear in the heart of the onlooker. As he went through the city, judgment from God like fireworks streaking across the sky, would shoot out the back of his chariot over the city. It struck terror in my heart!

We began to run from city to city; each time we entered into a new city, it seemed like the angel of the Lord would arrive just as we did. His mission was always the same, to bring judgment!

I then realized we were backtracking over the cities that we had previously visited. As we entered into the cities, I would attempt to perceive whether or not the angel of Judgment had been there. I thought, as we approached one city; oh the angel of the Lord has not been here. Immediately I had a vision of him standing at the gate of the city, releasing judgment over that city. So, we continued running. We came to another city, and I perceived that the angel had not been there. So, I said: "This city is not under the judgment of God, thus the Church is at peace and rest!" However, every city that we entered into that was under the judgment of God, nessecitated that we leave immediately.

As we were leaving one city that was under God's judgment, my brother Kenny wanted to linger to talk to the angel. But, I cried out to him: "Kenny, don't tarry ~ run, as this city is under God's judgment and we must leave here quickly!" Just then the angel of the Lord caught up with us, and seeing Kenny linger back to talk to him, he cried out: "Leave son of man, leave here quickly as God's judgment is upon this city!"

—— ✦ ——

10/94 A VISION

"A PEEK INTO REALITY"

I was at a friend's house and in prayer. I felt compelled to open my eyes and look at the wall in front me. As I did, I saw their piano, upon which sat a family portrait, and a lovely plant. Above the piano on the wall was a huge and lovely picture of Jesus.

As I looked to see what the Lord might be speaking to me, I realized that the only thing with life in it was the plant. Everything else was lifeless and without the power of life in any way. The contrast was so real and obvious that it shocked me. It was as though everything but the plant had become two dimensional while the plant remained three dimensional. I had never realized before that I thought these inanimate objects had life in them. Or that I thought that they had the power to somehow give life, or to in any way improve the quality of life. But, obviously I did, and that delusion lay in some deep part of my heart.

The Lord let me know that He had temporarily removed the veil of deception that lay over the whole world. It is the lie that anything outside of God has the power of life. It is so subtle we would never know that it exists if the Lord didn't reveal it by divine revelation.

Jesus said that Satan is the author of "the lie" not lies! That is the lie, the belief that anything outside of God can give or improve the quality of true life. Because of Adam and Eve's fall, we all see through this deceptive veil. Now it can only be removed through the work of the Holy Spirit in sonship. (John 6:63)

— ◆ —

2/95 A PROPHETIC DREAM

"WOE TO THE RICH"

The scene opened with me in a restaurant finishing a prophetic dance. I was then taken up into heaven to see momentarily behind the veil that I might give a message to the people I was standing before. When I returned, having been gone for just a moment, I asked my captive audience if they understood what I had just done. They simply stared at me looking very bewildered, not knowing what to say.

My audience consisted of upper-middle to upper class business people. The least wealthy was very wealthy. And, it was for this reason that God was speaking to them. I said: "I have just preformed a prophetic dance, speaking of God's judgement which is even now coming upon you!" Just then, a woman who was sitting behind me, and to my left, began to mock me. I turned, looking straight at her, and pointed my finger at her, saying: "You will not mock God!" She immediately fell dead.

I turned back around crying out to the whole audience: "You thought God gave you all your great wealth to pour out on all your lusts. You spent your money on whatever your passion might crave, that is what you wanted, and that is what you bought. Large homes, expensive clothing, alcohol, fancy and expensive automobiles ~ on and on it goes ~ whatever you craved, that is what you bought. This you did while the poor and the afflicted and the needy sat outside your door in want of necessities. Them you sent away empty!

Just then a man began to mock me. I turned to him pointing my finger at him, and yelled: "What about you. God put millions of dollars into your hands, and you have repaid Him by spending it on loose women and expensive vacations, not to name a few of your extremities. "He immediately fell dead.

Just then another woman began to mock me. I turned toward her, pointing my finger straight at her, and directly rebuked her saying: "And what about you; whose god is your alcohol?" She immediately dropped dead.

By this time I was shaken. Why are these people dying? I thought. Notwithstanding, I continued to speak to these hard-hearted people. "God gave you that wealth to provide for the needs of the poor and needy. But, you have mocked God and His mercy by lavishing your abundance upon your own greedy lusts." Just then another man began to mock me. I quickly turned and looking straight at him with my finger pointed in his face: "What about you, whose money is your God?" He immediately died.

I turned around and lifted my hands in the air toward my Father in Heaven and cried: "Lord God of heaven and earth, if it has been You who has spoken through me and I am your servant, send thunder and lightening and a severe rain storm now!" Immediately, it began to rain in a frightening degree. The terror of the Lord fell on all the people, and they began to bow under the conviction of the Holy Spirit. They began to moan and mourn over their sins.

I awoke with the fear of the Lord still filling my heart. I was not able to move for an hour for the degree of the terror of the Lord that had encompassed me. Woe be to the rich who spend their wealth on the lust of their flesh instead of giving to the poor in these last days. The judgment of God is going to fall on the greedy in ways it has not done since the days of Noah. Luke, chapter six.

———— ✦ ————

2/95 A VISON

"THE SIN OF COVETOUSNESS"

I saw in a vision, that the sin of covetousness is equivalent to murder in God's eyes. I saw a woman take something that another woman wanted, because she wanted it so badly. Then I saw the same act from God's perspective. The woman wanted what the other woman wanted, so she took it not caring what the other felt. But, because the second woman did not want to let it go, the first woman lifted her hand and struck the second one down with a knife. I was in shocked horror at what I saw. So, I cried out: "Lord I must see this in your Word if I am ever to give it to your Church. Immediately He told me where to find it.

You are jealous and covet [what others have] and your desires go unfulfilled; [so] you become murderers. (James 4:2) This is why the sin of covetousness is denounced in the Ten Commandments. It is also the sin of self-idolatry. (Col. 3:5) Paul said in fact, that it is the fundamental sin from which springs every other sin. (I Tim. 6:10) Therefore my Dear Reader, we must as Christians flee this sin as though it were the plague.

———— ✦ ————

"PERVERSION IN THE CHURCH"

I was in worship this morning in Church, when the Lord compelled me to look out over the congregation. I was standing in the balcony. When I did look out over the scene before me, I saw the worship team, the choir, and the congregation all in worship. But, it looked like it was a rock concert. The longer I watched the more grievous it became. I was struck with horror at what I saw. The whole scene was a perversion of His holiness. It was full of flesh. It looked like people were deep in worship. But, the truth was their hearts were far from God, thinking about everything under the sun, but Him. The atmosphere was filled with perversion. I began to cry uncontrollably. The reality of how the Lord saw our worship was so painful, I just wept and wept. Others around me thought I was being touched by the Lord, but I was bent over in deep grief.

I rose back up, and looked out over the congregation again seeing the same thing, but this time the Holy Spirit came into the sanctuary. I cried to the Lord: "Why, why do You visit us in all this perversion?" He spoke so tenderly saying: *"I want my people to feel my love!"* I then asked Him what we must do to make our worship beautiful to Him. He replied: *"Worship me in spirit and in truth. What does that mean? Live a consecrated life. Be holy, and love your neighbor as you love yourself, and worship me from a pure heart!"*

———✦———

8/95 A DREAM OF INSTRUCTION

"JOSEPH"

I saw Joseph of Old Testament renown. The scene opened with Joseph riding up on a camel, to a clothier where he would ordinarily have purchased custom made clothes for himself to wear. He was wearing his coat of many colors and looked like a prince in his fine apparel. Further, he carried himself with dignity and nobility. Once he arrived in front of this mens' clothier, he dismounted his camel and walked in through the front door.

Then I noticed his brothers, who were around the side of the building. They were discussing Joseph among themselves. I could hear them discuss a plan to stay out of sight until Joseph came back out, at which time they would ambush him and kill him so they could steal his wealth. They waited for the longest time. But, Joseph never again came back out the front.

At length, I went around back and noticed a young man walking out the back door, he was dressed in the garb of a slave. I observed him closely for a few minutes before I realized that this young man was in fact, Joseph. He had gone in to the clothier's looking like a prince, which in fact he was, and walked out the back door looking like a humble servant. I continued to watch him as he unfastened a donkey that was in the back and began to walk away with him. Just out front, he stopped for a moment and checked the two saddlebags that were on his donkey. I noticed that he had some bottles of oil stored in them. By this means he looked like a peasant oil merchant. I also intuitively knew that he was carrying his great wealth under his clothes and secured by a belt.

After a few minutes he began to walk again heading down the path to his destination. So, I quietly followed him hoping to see what his brothers would do. As Joseph came around the front within eye-view, I heard one of the brothers say: "Wait a minute, who is that?" as he pointed at Joseph. Another of the brothers replied: "Oh, that is just a poor oil merchant." With that they turned around and continued to wait for Joseph to emerge through the front door.

As for Joseph, he walked on in safety, not being at all recognized by his treacherous brothers.

The Lord then spoke to me: *"The enemy cannot steal your wealth when you are clothed with humility."*

———— ✦ ————

"THE ANTI-CHRIST"

I saw a whole city of people go underground and into an underground city as they had just received news of the approach of the terrible king. This king was made of ice. (The Lord used this to depict the heart of ice that was in him.) He was about 12 feet in height and was in every way terrible in his appearance. When this king would speak, he spoke as it were with thunder, so much that the very earth would shake at the sound of his voice. He was known for his cruelty and was therefore greatly feared. As he would enter into a given city, he would send a man ahead to trumpet his coming. It was by this means that these underground city dwellers were alerted as to his approach, and scurried underground for safety.

As he arrived at the city center his scouts went in search of those who were hiding. As they were discovered they were forced out of hiding, and were made to come and kneel down before this mighty tyrant.

As some knelt they put beautiful pillows of tapestry under their knees to cushion themselves. When the king saw this he became very angry. In a violent rage he tore the pillows out from under them and told them to get out of his sight. As they stood to leave, I noticed that they were not dressed like the others. They were dressed in fine coats of many colors; which was indicative of their pride. As they departed from the king's presence, they would turn and sneer at him behind his back. The others obeyed the king and simply knelt down before him. I noticed that these were all dressed in servant's garb and were barefooted. This too bore a symbolism. It symbolized their humility.

The king then turned to one of those who were kneeling and commanded him to rise. As the Christian obeyed, the king commanded the young man to walk over and worship the king's idol. I knew the young man wouldn't do it because of his love for Christ. I also knew it would mean his death. Just as I suspected the young man politely refused. So the king demanded that he be killed immediately.

9/95 A WORD

"WORD OF WISDOM"

Just as I awoke, the Lord spoke to me audibly. He said: *"Among the foxes come the more enlightened ones."* May we beware!

——— ✦ ———

10/95 A VISION

"CRUSHING OF THE ROSES"

In a vision, I saw an elderly gentleman that I recognized as being a prophet, standing on a street corner selling crushed roses. A man came up to him and said: "What are you crazy, who would want to buy crushed roses?" The prophet replied: "Oh, the roses must be crushed to bring out the full beauty of their irrepressible fragrance. It is God's way."

——— ✦ ———

1/96 A VISION

"JESUS ANNOUNCES REVIVAL"

While in Church, during worship, I felt compelled to look up into the balcony on the other side of the building. As I did, I saw Jesus standing there. He spoke to me saying: *"Prepare ye; prepare ye the way of the Lord, for the day of the Lord's visitation is close at hand. It will be a day of blessing, a day when the righteous will be separated from the unrighteous, a day of salvation, and a day of judgment."*

——— ✦ ———

12/96 A DREAM

"IN REFORM"

I saw in a dream, God's response to our repentance, and how God watches over our reform. Then came the words: *"And He saw that they constantly disobeyed him in the wilderness. But, as God became tender toward their reform, He healed them."*

———— ✦ ————

2/96 A VISION

"VEILS"

I saw myself in a vision, walking through this long hall of beautiful veils. They were all in colors of the rainbow. For instance, one was pastel pink, another was violet, ect. Between each veil, the walls one either side of the corridor were the color of the preceding veil. It was so lovely. The veils were all transparent in their appearance also. It seemed like I walked forever through these veils. But, with each veil I would go through, the understanding and spiritual vision of the Lord and His kingdom would become clearer and clearer, which brought great joy to my heart. The further I walked the more clearly I could see God's glory until His glorious and radiant throne stood before me. These are veils of the flesh life.

———— ✦ ————

5/96 A PROPHETIC DREAM

"VICTORY OVER THE STRONGMEN"

The Lord graciously sought to comfort and encourage me as I had been through many horrific battles with the enemy which I didn't understand.

Consequently Jesus chose to speak to me through a powerful prophetic dream, which would also serve to give me understanding of the past battles.

The Dream:

I was in the heavenlies fighting strongmen. While engaged in this battle, I kept tumbling, seemingly out of control and at the control of an unseen force. Irrespective of the immense confusion I was feeling, I took down one strongman after another. After I had taken down many strongmen, I was feeling pretty dazed. Just as suddenly as it began, it was over, and I was standing erect on an invisible floor.

I then climbed down a small and invisible flight of stairs entering a Church congregation. On my way down, I saw all the strongmen that I had conquered looking for seats in the congregation, for they were now a defeated foe. They were disarmed and completely harmless.

As I descended into the congregation, I heard a multitude of voices say: "You brought down all the principalities that hinder the Church, but two!" These victories were personal victories, which must be gained before a person can gain them for anyone else. So, these principalities are disarmed as to my ministry, and me. I therefore can walk in an anointing to help set other willing souls free. Although, I have since, been tempted by these evil spirits, they have no power over me, and will never again, as long as I continue seeking humility, meekness and purity. The Lord then caused me to know that this in fact, is the process in which, all the mighty men of valor are presently engaged; and that we are very close to the end of our battle. Therefore, the day of the anointing is close at hand. Further, when we are living a life of true religion instead of under the guise of a religious spirit, strongholds are brought down through the purity of our lives.

As I awoke, it was revealed to me that the whole book of James fully clarifies true religion against living under the auspices of a religious spirit. Subsequently, I began an in-depth study on the book of James and found the revelation to be true.

———— ✦ ————

"THE SPIRIT OF THE WORLD"

In a dream, my daughter Ricci and I were on a trip, and were running from one restaurant to another looking for some decent food, so we could continue down the road. We then walked into what we hoped would be our final choice. We took our liberty and sat down in a booth and began to look at the menu. After looking over the menu, and before ordering, I decided to visit the ladies room. After I was finished, I headed back to our table. On my way, a man whose intent it was to rape me, ran into me. But, when I yelled out for help, it frightened him, so he ran away. I again headed back for our table and my daughter, who at that time was only 11 years old. As I was re-entering the dining room, the waitress came up to me and reported to me: "You have overcome everyone in this room, but one. That one is the woman sitting at the food bar. Watch out for her, as she is the worst of all. She is the "spirit of harlotry".

I continued back to the table where my daughter was sitting. As I came near the table, the woman I had been warned about started to stagger toward our table. (This woman by the way, looked just like Harriet Nelson, from the Ozzie and Harriet fame.) She was utterly intoxicated. As she approached our table, I blurted out: "you look just like Harriet Nelson. She simply smiled a cynical smile. It was her smile that opened my eyes to see that she was the "spirit of the world" that I had been warned about. Further, I realized that she wore both titles. The spirit of the world and the spirit of harlotry are one in the same.

I then looked at Ricci and demanded: "Let's go honey ~ now!" We immediately began to prepare to leave. I was by now standing, while Ricci was getting ready to stand. As the woman saw this, she began to wedge herself in between Ricci and myself. She was trying desperately to force herself between us and keep Ricci from being able to stand. **"No!"** I cried, and pushed her out of the way, took Ricci by the hand and we left.

Immediately upon awakening the Lord began to speak to me. He showed me three things. First: one of the two spirits I have yet to conquer is the "spirit of the world, or harlotry." It was this one with which the mighty men of valor and I were now in battle and being called to overcome.

Secondly: I was so aware of her drunkenness which was repulsive to me. I asked the Lord, with what was she drunk? He answered immediately. *"She is drunk with the blood of the saints!"*

Third: the spirit of harlotry doesn't look like a harlot. She looks like the ideal housewife and mother. This was to point out that the spirit of harlotry represented any life or thing in life that was not fully depended upon God. No matter how good and ethical it may look, if it isn't a life in full dependence upon the Lord, it is the spirit of harlotry or spirit of the world, as they are one in the same. We must learn to fear with great fear, the life of self-sufficiency, independent and autocratic rule; the life of sovereignty, the life of self-government, as it is the fountainhead of the spirit of harlotry. So, though we may be saved, if we are not walking in union with Christ, we are still albeit, unbeknownst to us, drinking from the bloody cup of the spirit of harlotry. This is where the Church is today, and so few realize it. The life we live with Christ looks both innocent, and natural, but it is a constant working of death, because it is not fully His life from which we are drinking. Though we have been blind to it in the past, we must now awaken to the truth, let it heal us, and flee this spirit before it destroys us. In conclusion, if we desire to be part of the bride of Christ in this life, we must flee this spirit, as no one can enter into the union with Christ with this spirit in their heart. (Revelation 17: 15 - 18:15)

—— ✦ ——

6/96 A DREAM

"THE SPIRIT OF THE WORLD"

The second dream I had that same night was as follows. I was talking to a Christian friend as we sat in her living room. I was telling her that I had seen the spirit of the world. She seemed basically disinterested. So, I asked her: "You do know what the spirit of the world is, don't you?" She replied: "No!" I then instructed her that it is the spirit of harlotry found in Revelation 17:15 — 18:15. Then I got up and walked out.

When I re-entered the room, she was sitting in front of the television wearing a modern hairdo and long dangly earrings, and a very up to date and faddish outfit. She depicted the epitome of the adult Christian who had not severed themselves from the spirit of the world and was therefore still living for the world. This was not a life of gross sin, just a love for the ways, fads and customs of the world. It also signifies those still living in their own sovereignty.

———— ✦ ————

5/96 A VISION

"THE GOLDEN ROAD"

I had just finished ministering and we had moved back into worship to prepare for the ministry service. I saw a vision. I saw thousands of people at the crosswalk of life. The path they were on was a dirt road, but they were standing at a place where two roads meet. The road that faced them was paved with gold. It was marked "the highway of holiness." The Lord spoke to me: *"Keep calling My people from the highways and byways of this life, to walk the road of holiness."* I then looked at the top of the road and saw stationed, the throne of Jesus. As the Lord spoke these words, I saw these multitudes of people turning from the path of their sojourn and walking onto the "highway of holiness."

———— ✦ ————

6/96 A VISION

"THE GOLDEN CHALLIS"

I saw a golden challis with liquid love beginning to bubble up until it overflowed the rim. Quickly, it turned into a smooth and abundant stream of golden liquid love, flowing out to the Church. This is what is coming.

———— ✦ ————

7/96 A VISION

"CANKER WORMS"

I saw in a vision, that when a Christian continues to chase after the things of the world, that it leaves the door wide open for the canker worms to eat away at our righteousness.

———— ✦ ————

7/96 A VISION

"THE OVERCOMERS"

As the scene opened in this prophetic dream, there were about a dozen of us running through a huge single story mansion. We were running with all our might desperately trying to find the way out. This mansion looked like it was about 20,000 square feet or more. It seemed like it was a house with no end. In structure, it most resembled a California ranch. But, there seemed to be endless passageways throughout the house.

We had been taken there by force, but we were determined to get out regardless of the cost. Getting out was proving to be no easy task however. As I mentioned, there were endless passageways through which we could find endless doors, but not all doors would aid us in getting free from this house. In fact, most doors were simply dead-end sites leading nowhere or worse yet, doors leading to rooms of entrapment. So, we quickly learned that we needed to be careful. We seemed to know intuitively which door would prove to be detrimental, and which door would work to our advantage. Consequently we were able to be very careful not to try to go through the wrong door wasting precious time, or bringing an end to our quest by getting trapped.

As we would happen upon a door that we intuitively knew would bring us one door closer to freedom, we would silently look at each other, all knowing simultaneously that it was correct, and would burst through it together. By this means we would use our united strength to break through otherwise impervious doors into the next area of conquest. Once we broke through the new door, we would run down the new corridor looking for the next door. Again we would find ourselves running by an endless maze of doors which we knew would avail us nothing, until we would happen upon the next door that we knew would be a valuable exit from the corridor. As we would run down each new hallway, we would have to turn many corners, avoid many other turns, leaping over obstacles, running around other obstacles, and forcing out of our path still other seemingly immovable obstacles. We were constantly trying to avoid things that would seem to fly right out of the wall at us, trying to hit and injure us. Nothing was able to hinder our advance, as we all had set our face like flint to be free. There were times that we would be very weary, but we didn't dare stop or even slow down, as we knew the owner of the house had an army running after us trying to find and detain us from our freedom. Further, he had others that were attempting to set ambushes against us at critical doors, so even slowing down would put us in grave danger.

At long last, the front door of this great sprawling mansion was in view. We knew that if we could get through that door, we would be out of the house, with only the front gate of the property being left to penetrate. Once outside the gate we would be free and the owner of the house could not touch us again.

By the time we reached the view of the front door; which in itself looked more like an entrance to a prison, than a house, the owner of the house knew for certain that we were about to escape. We could hear him over the intercom, giving instructions to his host of guards at the two doors. He was yelling at them to stop us at all cost, even if it meant killing us to keep us from escaping. They were told to use every weapon available to them to stop our progress or end our lives. The owner didn't really seem to care which alternative the guards used, only that we were stopped from escaping. His merciless and determined commands riddled the air at times sending shivers down our spines as they bombarded the airwaves. But, we didn't dare let fear impede us to any degree. We had to keep running. As we came nearer the front door, the guards began to bombard us with huge darts that looked more like ice-picks in size. Some were poisonous, but all had the ability to kill in one way or other. We were able to successfully evade each one however, as we would serpentine around them, often just barely missing them. Finally at the entrance, we all looked at each other, and knew that in order to make it through those huge doors we would have to use our collective strength, hitting it head on with all our might at precisely the same moment. As we would blow them open we would have to use the momentum we had gained to hit the front gates just as hard to make it through them as they too were steel. So, we mustard together all of our strength, energy and concentration for the attack. We then began to be barraged by the guards with every kind of weapon they had in an attempt to stop us. Their ammunition pounded us with a furry, but we knew we couldn't pay any attention, as all our thoughts, energy, and efforts had to be used to break through the steel door and gate.

As agreed, we all hit the door simultaneously with such force the door blew open, and we were in the courtyard, just moments from freedom.

Now we all riveted our focus onto the finale quest, knowing that we would have only one chance to make it through that gate. The owner of the house himself knew we were about to get away as he was monitoring the battle. Desperate, he began to shout demands at a rapid pace. He ordered more guards to the front courtyard. Then he screamed that more artillery must be brought in and used against us. His demands were immediately met. Thus we fell under greater firing than ever before. They used guns, flaming missiles and sent strange looking daggers flying at us. Still others began to chase us with huge knives. I heard the owner of the estate yell: "If you don't stop them, I will have you all killed! You kill them, or you are dead! Kill them, kill them, don't let them escape!"

But, we were able to successfully dodge ever effort, albeit oft times just barely getting away. We all looked at each other one last time to synchronize our efforts, thoughts and energies in order to make the united and concentrated bolt through the heavy steel gate. We then looked at the gate and blasted it with all our united strength. In just a moment, we were flying in the wings of freedom, much to the owner's rage and dismay. We left him behind, ranting and raving at his unexpected loss. But, we were free! I awoke.

The Lord immediately spoke to me, letting me know that these were the mighty men of valor, and that we were at this time heading toward the door of the great house. The enemy is out to kill, so we need to run circumspectly and with all fervor!

You may ask why none of us spoke verbally to one another. It is because in reality, none of us, knows who the other is. So, although we are all at the same place in preparation, we are all strangers to one another according to the flesh. Yet, by the Holy Spirit's own marvelous grace, He has brought us all to the same place at the same time. Soon we will be totally free of the spirit of the world, and free to help others get the same liberty.

—— ✦ ——

"REVIVAL AMONG THE CHILDREN"

In the afternoon, the Lord spoke to me saying: "Write the vision, and make it plain upon the tablets, that he may run that readeth it." (Habakkuk 2:20) As my Savior spoke thus to me, I was flooded with tears of love for the vision. "But what vision?" I asked.

Then about midnight, I was given three visions. Each one spoke of the same thing, only the scene changed.

First vision: I was standing in the hall between two Sunday school rooms. Both of these rooms were filled with children at the time. Suddenly, the power of God came down so hard and so fast that all of us, teachers, children and myself went down under His descending power. All of us were totally unconscious. When I revived, I asked about the condition of the children. The teachers having revived also by that time, made a count of the children and their spiritual state, asking also what happened to them while they were under the Lord's power.

One teacher reported that three children in one room and five in another room had just given their lives to Jesus. Nearly all the children were baptized in the Holy Spirit. Several had received visions of the Lord and several others were taken to heaven for a visit.

Second vision: I was opening the doors of a Church, which immediately filled with children. The Lord's power descended upon us, and all the children fell out under His power simultaneously. It was an extraordinary visitation. Again, many were saved, many more were filled with the Holy Spirit, and many received visions of various sorts. Some visions were of heaven, others of hell, still others of Jesus or angels.

Then I received a third vision. I was again instructing children. Hundreds of children were present. I was recanting a recent visitation of the Lord as He had visited children. I extended my arms and bent down as though doing knee bends to demonstrate what I was sharing. Suddenly, the power of the Lord came in during my demonstration. As I bent down in demonstration, He descended on these children to whom I was speaking. All of us went out. Again, the harvest of souls was abundant, with perhaps a third of the children getting saved. Nearly all were baptized in the Holy Spirit, and again, many of the children were given visions. They received visions of heaven, hell, angels and the Lord! All this took place with absolutely no human intervention. It was a simple matter of God invading the human heart. It was extraordinarily wonderful.

—— ◆ ——

8/96 A VISION

"TWO VISIONS

A voice spoke these words: "The sheep's wool will be sheared, but that is good as the sheep are supposed to produce wool. The sheep will be sheared that some that have none may have a little and those who have some may have more. This spoke of the persecution of the saints.

The second vision: I parked my compact car and went with an angel into a bomb shelter that was quite amazing. It was almost a luxury shelter. After my tour, I returned to my automobile to leave. But, I kept bumping into a fence that was at the rear of my car. My automobile which aforetime could turn on a dime was now turning like a truck. Further, my car would stop on a dime, but now it would barely stop at all when once put into motion. Feeling totally frustrated, I decided to just sit still for a few minutes. Sitting there behind the wheel, I began looking around and spotted another angel sitting on a rather unusual piece of equipment. It seemed he was helping to make another bomb shelter. I just sat there watching him for a moment. Having noticed me, the angel stopped what he was doing, and turned around to talk to me.

He said: "You should see the special games your enemies are planning. Believe me, your leaders are going to need these shelters." So, these shelters were not for the common people, but only the dignitaries. As he shared, he seemed troubled and angry. He kept emphasizing the seriousness of their barbaric plans. That is when I realized why he was angry. He was distraught because the common people were not being made aware of the horrific plans and made provision for in the time of trouble.

I couldn't help but notice the unusual piece of equipment he was sitting on, thus my curiosity was aroused. So, I asked him what it did. He responded with: "Oh this thing, it can do a sixteenth of an inch work making the walls of the shelter velvety smooth." The vision then came to an end.

The meaning: Our temporal help is going to be totally ineffective when their games begin. Further, our dignitaries care only about their own protection, and do not care in the least about the needs of the common people. Their own shelters are elaborate and more than sufficient for the days of trouble. But, the common people have nothing. The angel of the Lord was in no way pleased that the common people are being blindly lead to slaughter, while the political aristocracy gorge themselves in luxury.

8/96 A DREAM

"A DREAM OF WARNING"

I had just preached a message to an audience in which sat an old prophetess. Afterwards she came up to me to chat. In the course of our conversation, she offered: "We could make up a demonstration tape and have one of your messages on it, and one of mine. We could send out about three tapes a week in packages to pastors to get some meetings scheduled. She offered this idea several times in the course of our conversation. However, I tried to ignore it, as I knew she had become terribly impure and was on her way down. For God himself was bringing an end to her ministry.

Finally she said: "Your message was terribly hard hitting, I felt conviction several times." Because I cared about her as a person, I agreed to visit with her a while longer at her home. So, we arose and went to get in her car. As we approached her automobile, I thought; my, this Cadillac is exquisite, and quite a luxury car, but I said nothing. We got in and drove to her home. After a short drive we arrived at her home which was also very beautiful. It had all the special touches to make it homey, but elegant. It took my breath away. I was so surprised to see that she lived in such luxury. I thought to myself as I looked around; my, she has everything a person could ever want, the best of everything. Then I thought; but she has no ministry left and no anointing. Boy, what a price!

———— ✦ ————

5/96 A REVELATION

"A HEAVENLY REVELATION"

I began to learn in 1989 that the Lord will take us through tests in our Christian walk just as He did Abraham. These tests are to determine whether or not we are worthy to receive a promise He has made or a blessing He would like to bestow upon us. We will never know that we are being taken through a test however, until we have passed or failed, and only if Jesus wants to reveal it to us. For instance, if He wants to bestow a certain blessing, He may ask us if we are willing to walk through a certain kind of trial, or to relinquish our right to something that seems dear to us. In the Lord's question, He will not necessarily share the blessing He is desiring to bestow for yielding on a certain issue, He will only make His request known. If we yield, He will then share the blessing He had intended to give. If we do not, He will never as a rule, tell us what we lost in our decision. It will simply remain a lost blessing. The same is true of tests that our Master may take us through in regards to promises He has already made. Such was the case with Abraham in the call to sacrifice Isaac.

With that understanding in mind, I will share with you a special blessing the Lord gave to me. The main reason I am sharing it however, is that in my blessing came a beautiful revelation for any who are desirous of becoming part of the bride of Christ.

I was taken through a very painful trial, not in the least knowing that it was a test. Neither did I know at the time that the promise of union with Christ for which I had waited and longed for a great length of time was on the line. I was simply ushered through this test, with the potential of failure at many different junctures. The only reason I didn't fail was because my Master had taught me so well in previous years how to go through similar situations. At each juncture I had decisions to make, and although I was in a great deal of pain making the right decision extremely difficult to enact, still I knew the right thing to do, and I wouldn't have done otherwise. By the end of this trial which lasted for about ten days or so, I would end up being in utter amazement at the goodness of the Lord and how He protected me against the work of those who had made themselves an enemy to me. Love prevailed in the situation, and God brought my enemy to shame, through much sorrow on my part. I didn't desire my enemy hurt, or for him to be brought to shame, but, I did marvel at how God protected me.

The night my trial came to an end, I was pleased that as difficult as it was to do right at the last juncture, that I had found the grace to sacrifice myself, for the sake of my enemy. I was pleased, as I knew that my Father was pleased.

When I went to bed that night, I was in awe of God. I had laid down my life, but He chose not to take the sacrifice and gave it back to me. I could hardly believe my Savior and Redeemer's wonderful goodness. When I finally fell asleep, I was still wrapped in the Lord's presence. Then I had a wonderful dream from my Master. This dream seemed like it was right out of Disney, for the way it was portrayed to me.

The Dream: I was walking down a long, narrow, and winding path, for the purpose of finding the prince with whom I was to be wed. This path wound through a very thick and dark forest which, by the way was part of the Kingdom owned by my arch-enemy. I walked ahead of several others who were there for the express purpose of following me.

I was continually intercepted all along the way, by various forest creatures. Their purposes in intercepting me would vary, as it would depend on the reason they had individually been sent by the king of the forest. But, all the creatures had come in one fashion or another, intermittently throughout my journey for the express purpose of prohibiting me from finding the valuable key that I was there to find. It was necessary to find this key if I was ever to hope to bring the prince out of hiding in order for the marriage to be consummated. As I already mentioned, their purposes would vary, some, particularly the small creatures such as rabbits, birds, squirrels and even such as the deer would come in an attempt to distract me from my journey. Others such as elk, bears, and even lions would come for the purpose of trying to take my life. The evil king, who owned them, however was sending them all.

I overcame every attempt made by his ambassadors; as I had but one purpose for being in this forest; that was to find the valuable key that would unlock my future with the prince whom I loved with all my heart. At length, I came to an opening upon which the path opened up and came to an end. It was like a cul-de-sac in the middle of the forest. As I came upon it, I began to realize that this key was hidden somewhere in this opening. With great earnest, I set out to find it, as I knew without this key, my future would not be with my beloved prince. I began to search around the edge of the clearing, and in the surrounding thicket, shrubs and trees for the key. My companions remained with me all this time. I searched and searched. All the while a ball of blue light kept coming at me from different places around this clearing. It would come at me with lightening speed, from first one place then another. I never knew from which direction it would come, so I had to be very watchful and careful, even while I looked for the key. I instinctively knew that if this ball hit any of us, we would immediately die. So, I had to be sure to catch it, so that it wouldn't hit any of my company.

When I caught the ball, I would have to send it back to the same place in the thicket, for had I done otherwise, there would always be the chance of hitting something which would cause it to bounce back hitting someone in my company and killing them. Yet, each time I would send the ball back to his cave, the evil king would secretly send it to one of hidden soldiers who would throw it at me from another location. The war continued in this way for a while, which prompted me to begin to try to find the king, so I could confront him personally. Yet, I also continued desperately searching for the key that would unlock the whereabouts of my prince and compel him to come forward.

Suddenly, I realized that this king must be in a certain cave. So, I moved toward this cave in hope of spotting him. Then I saw him. He was a huge rat that stood upright, and communicated as a man. Upon seeing him, I said: "Oh, he's nothing but an ugly old rat." Having finally discovered him, I kept looking trying to see what it was he was trying so hard to hide. Suddenly, I spotted something behind him. It looked like something was being hidden in a treasure chest that was clothed in light. I looked still closer, then I realized that it was the key I had been looking for. It was sitting in this open chest, and was covered by a protective dome of light. It was exceedingly beautiful. I gasped: "GOODNESS!" The king rat looked around in shock. He cried: "What! ~ What did she say?" I replied with sheer delight: "GOODNESS, that is the brides name!" The rat then knew that I had just discovered the vital key and that he had lost. The prince would now come forward and we would be wed. The dream came to an end, and I awoke.

As I awoke the Holy Spirit swept through me and spoke to me. He said: "You were just taken through a critical test and you passed. Goodness has overcome evil, Nita!" My whole room was lit up with the glow of heaven, and it seemed as though the very heavens had been opened to me to have a special momentary communion with my divine Prince which lasted for a couple of hours. Because I had just passed this critical test, the union for which I had waited was now a sealed promise. Nothing short of my own turning away would prohibit it from occurring. My heart was so filled with divine love, even for the one who had become a Judas to me. I had a new love for him, which was way beyond what I had held for him the many years of our friendship. I felt so tender, like a protective nurturing mother toward him. Yet, at the same time I was so filled with the joy of my heavenly Father. He was proud of me, and I knew it. He was so happy for me, and I knew that also, as all this was rushing through my heart. I spent some time praying for my lost friend, and then spent some more time worshipping my Lord, then eventually went back to sleep.

The main reason I shared this very private experience was to encourage you. It was difficult to open such a sacred thing and let you share it with me. But, I chose to do it, for your sake, my Dear Reader. Any one who would become part of the bride of Christ must enter into this divine goodness in dealing with others, friend or foe. God requires it, albeit, not without providing the grace, and the power to enter therein.

So, please be encouraged, and let all of your dealings with others be out of the deepest love, because Christ has first loved us.

———— ✦ ————

9/96 A VISION

"TWO ARMIES"

As I was on a walk with a friend, I looked into the sky and saw the sky nearly black with vultures. I looked again and they were gone. Then the Lord said: *"after the vultures will come the white eagles to heal My people."*

———— ✦ ————

9/96 A VISION

"A WORD FROM THE LORD"

In a vision I was given a powerful word from the Lord. As the Lord spoke it, the words would be printed out on a text and illuminated with light. At the end of this personal word, He then spoke a word for the Church. He said: "There are over 900 names revealing My character in the Bible, all of which are poorly represented by my Church." I also read this as He spoke it to me. I felt the utter unworthiness of the whole Church, myself included, to be graced with even the smallest revelation of even one of His names. Yet, beyond my comprehension, I knew I was being lifted up and united to these revelations. I could actually feel Him uniting me to this purpose and experience as His holiness began to fill my whole being. The vision then came to an end,.

Moments later, the whole vision replayed. Only this time, I was lifted up off the bed and taken into a place of God's jealousy and wrath. In this place there are thunders and lightening constantly going off. His holiness again filled my inner-most being, and again the Lord spoke to me about our unworthiness to receive these revelations, and how we have so poorly misrepresented His names. However, this time the emphasis was on my unworthiness. He then revealed to me how I had disobeyed Him in a very simple matter that to me had seemed insignificant. That was why I wondered if it was the Lord that had commanded me thus.

As He showed me this disobedience, His thunderings and lightening entered my spirit, wounding me. Then I understood that this was a place of God's judgment, and He had judged my sin. I further learned from this that no disobedience is minor to the Lord. I cried out to Him, telling Him how sorry I was, and wept for awhile. Then I just lay quiet for awhile in His presence meditating on what had just happened.

---- ✦ ----

10/96 A VISITATION

"JESUS OUR HIGH PRIEST"

Tonight during the worship service, while ministering in Hawaii, Jesus appeared to me as the faithful High Priest. He was dressed in the garb of the Old Testament High Priest. I saw Him walk back and forth across the platform. As He entered, so did a most wonderful presence of His Spirit. Most of us were on the floor to varying degrees, but all were in an elevated state of true spiritual worship. This worship wasn't something we had worked up, but was a gift of His wonderful grace. He looked beautiful in His High Priestly robe. As the Mediator of a better covenant, He watches over the development of our faith with scrupulous care. He allows us to partake of Himself and sees to it that nothing enters into our life without first passing through His own government. That is why He came, He came to encourage our faith and reveal a deeper dimension of Himself. This was His instruction. And, He came with great joy, sharing in our infirmities and bearing our sorrows with us. I was sent out to Hawaii on this trip knowing that I was going to meet with a great many storms.

Jesus had revealed this to me in several dreams, and words through others. So, He came, a Comfort in the midst of the storm. When He left, I was lifted into a higher grace. What a Friend I have in my Savior. What a wonderful Friend we all have in Him. Perhaps this would be a good time to just sit back and praise Him. For He is there, always there whether we see Him or we do not. He is right there to walk with us through every storm until He brings us out to a place of overcoming.

---- ◆ ----

11/96 A DREAM

"TIDAL WAVE"

Dream One: I saw a huge tidal wave rise straight up out of the ocean. It was a lava like substance; but had the force and the power of a tidal wave of water. As I saw it jet straight up into the sky, in shocked amazement, I cried: "That is what I saw in the vision! We must get to safety! It is coming out of an earthquake."

Initially, it didn't affect the house we were living in, so we grew slothful. Instead of rushing to safety, we continued to sit where we were and just look at the house. Then suddenly, it came crashing down on the house utterly demolishing it. I awoke.

Dream Two: This dream began where the other left off. The house we were in was in Michigan. It was very large, therefore had been converted to a nice apartment house. I was walking through the rubbish and debris of the wreckage from the tidal wave of lava that had destroyed it. In late morning, we received a call from a California anchorman wanting some technical understanding as to why the effects of the tidal wave had been so devastating. I couldn't answer his questions and I wanted to keep looking for people amidst the wreckage, so I turned him over to my father. As I walked away, I could hear my father say: "Well, the construction of the house was not that good to begin with, and then it was never repaired."

In this dream, the Lord of course was speaking about the Church. The foundation and structure of the modern Church continues to be in want of repair, but the Church is unwilling to make the needed repairs to their faith. We want dainty morsels not the message of the Cross, which is the only thing that will fix the problem. When the Satanic avalanche comes, those in the church who have refused the teachings of the Cross will be demolished, much to this Seer's sorrow.

Dream three: In a vision, I had seen bombs falling on a school in Edmonton, Alberta. Consequently, I busied myself with trying to warn everyone I could get to listen. Later I was talking to a friend about it as he seemed to be taking the things I was saying seriously. At one point in our conversation, I could hear his wife outside laughing with some friends. So, I walked over to the window to watch her. I then became discouraged, because not even my dear friend would listen to my repeated warnings, but continued to party with her friends. How would she make it, I thought. I turned to walk back to the desk where her husband was waiting to finish our conversation, and realized that he too was discouraged for he wanted so badly to have his wife listen. Before we could even make the next statement to finish our talk, the bombs began to fall.

Dream Four: I was now back in the States trying to warn every one to prepare for the Satanic tidal wave that was fast approaching. I went door to door in this Christian community, but no one would listen. The Christians would pray and believe God for this thing or that, and He would graciously respond to their prayers and provide, so they felt everything was all right. For this reason, they had no desire to listen to my pleadings. They would respond in such a casual way, not at all stirred to be careful about their souls. "Everything will be fine, God always answers our prayers. We'll be all right, you'll see."

Later, while down on the beach feeling so discouraged as I pondered the responses of people, I looked up to see who was making all the ruckus and saw a couple whom I had tried to warn earlier. They were wind surfing. I sat there watching them for a few minutes before they recognized me. When they did, they gleefully shouted out to me: "See, God will take care of everything. He won't let us get hurt!"

With that I began to weep before the Lord. "Lord, no one will listen to me, the tidal wave is coming, and no one is prepared." I knew so many would greatly suffer because they wouldn't listen. Others would be needlessly lost, because they shunned the strong warnings. I once again looked at the ocean where I had seen the tidal wave rise in the vision. When suddenly, the tidal wave I was trying to warn everyone about began to jet straight up out of the ocean.

———◆———

12/96 A VISITATION

"TURN FROM THE WORLD"

I was praying, wondering what the Lord would desire the central theme in my messages to be for 1997. When I saw the Lord standing to my right. To His right, and to my left was the world. Jesus looked at the world, then to me, and said: *"Nita, call My people out of the world. Tell them to leave the world and the things of the world and press into Me."* As He spoke, I saw such deep concern in His eyes. He was filled with compassion for His people and wanted very badly to see them in a place of safety in Himself. I could sense His deep yearning care for His own. Then He left.

———◆———

12/96 A VISION

"A WARNING"

I had a vision just as I was waking up in the morning. In the vision, my daughter and I were getting ready to go to sleep for the night. We had both been reading just before retiring, but, was now ready to turn the lights off and go to sleep. So, we rolled over to simultaneously turn our lights off. Nearly asleep, the Lord awakened me, by speaking to me from heaven. *"Some of the worst times in the history of mankind are going to take place during this administration."* I sat up with a start, and reached out to protect my daughter. Then in desperation my thoughts ran to other family members wanting to protect them. Be prayerful church, and walk circumspectly before God.

The Lord revealed this to me, for I had mumbled to Him just before retiring that night: "I feel that all the things I have seen won't happen for many years, so why, I complained: "am I driving myself so hard trying to reach people who don't want to be reached?"

——— ✦ ———

1/97 A VISION

"GOLD IN THE WORD"

As the scene opened, two of My friends, who incidentally were man and wife, were scuffling around in their back yard. It was evening and growing darker outside. They had jackets on because the weather was cool, as it was late fall. They were talking back and forth, as they scuffled around in this woodpile picking up first one piece of wood, then another, examining it and comparing it with something the man had in his hand, then throwing it down and going after the next piece of wood.

I was inside the house having just finished cleaning up when I realized that they both had gone outside. So, I decided to go outside and see what it was that they were looking for with such diligence. The husband then showed me a brick of pure gold he was holding in his hand. He then shared with me that a black man had come into his yard and handed this gold to him telling him that he had in fact picked it up in their own back yard. I looked at him quizzically and asked him where the man said that he found the gold. In answer to my question, he pointed to the back of the property, which was quite large and said: "Over there."

I then started heading in the direction he pointed out and my friends followed me. I continued to lead the way until we arrived at a tiny doorway in the side of a mountain that backed on to his property. It looked like an old abandon gold mine from the outside, but inside the walls were solid gold. As I leaned down into the opening, I heard a voice say: *"Come inside, its wonderful in here."* I peeked further inside, but was afraid to go in. I feared that it might be fools gold and that covetousness might have been what led me to go inside. If that would be true, I was terrified, I would be forever trapped, unable to get free to find the real gold of the Kingdom. The walls shined with such a beautiful light of golden glory, I wanted it to be of the Lord so badly, for its beauty. Not because I wanted earthly dust, but because I cherished the heavenly gold, and to think that it was here at my fingertips, I could hardly bear it. In the end, I decided not to take the chance.

As I stood in the entrance, it seemed to be the size of a man. But, as we were walking away, I turned back for one last look and saw that the entrance was the size of a mouse hole. That was why my friends were unable to go in, they couldn't get small enough. I then knew for sure that it was of the Lord; so I said: "It is of God and its all right!" Then I awoke.

What does it mean? We will never find the kingdom gold, rummaging around in the woodpile of the world. Only the refinement of God's holiness making us humble, meek and worthy of His gold will allow us the privilege of entering into the rich caverns of heaven's gold already laid in store for us. Only when we are small in our own eyes and fully free of the love of the world, will we even recognize it when we see it. Only then will we understand its great worth.

---- ✦ ----

4/97 A VISION

"REVIVAL IN EDMONTON ALBERTA"

While in the pulpit, I saw a vision of revival in Edmonton. Drug pushers, pimps, prostitutes, alcoholics, the worst of the worst of societies outcasts were brought into the kingdom and fully redeemed from their old life. Glorious miracles of every sort were taking place. God shook the whole city for Christ. Untold multitudes were getting saved. I saw it sweep right through the downtown area like a flood flowing through the streets!

———— ✦ ————

5/96 A WORD

"JUDGEMENT FOR CANADA"

Precisely on this day, (4-20-97) the Lord spoke to me telling me that that day would begin the cycle of judgment upon Canada. I shared that from the pulpit that morning. A man from the congregation came to me in the evening service and told me that indeed it had begun as they had experienced unprecedented flooding in the province of Manitoba. There was considerable damage done by the floods. This calamity as it turned out, led to others of equal severity. This is but a beginning however, so we must keep Canada in our prayers.

The Lord further shared these things.
1. Financial market will be unstable and is on its way to serious trouble.
2. Uprising against the government soon to break forth.
3. Eventual food shortages, which will ultimately become very severe.
4. Plagues.
5. Serious shaking in government.
6. Economic crunch causing severe decrease in living standards.
7. War.
8. Persecution coming against Christians and Jews.
9. Revival sweeping across the country to strengthen and stabilize the Christians for the time of persecution.

———— ✦ ————

"A PROPHETIC WARNING"

In this vision, I was standing by the ocean shore in southern California. I knelt down and holding a silver dollar in my fingers, I touched the water's edge, and looking behind me a great distance, said to my brother: "Someday, the ocean will own all of this." I was expressing that the ocean would own a considerable distance of what now was land. My thinking was that it would easily moved inland at least another mile of what was now land.

Just then, it was as though someone had burned a huge whole into another world. (It reminded me of the opening scene of a weekly movie from my childhood, by the name of Bonanza. Fire would burn a hole through the map of the Ponderosa exposing the Cartwrights all siting on their horses.) The veil just folded back as though it was being burned with fire. In just a moments time the hole was a good half a mile across and several stories high. What it exposed was incredible. I saw suspended over the ocean, what looked like miles of prairie. Running on the prairie, were hundreds of horses of every conceivable kind and color. Many were types of horses I had never before seen. Among the horses were cars from what may have been the 50s. They were all coming at me as fast as they could. No one was driving the cars, or riding the horses yet they were all moving forward at full speed. The whole scene was life size, so I would have been frightened had I not known that I was seeing the future. Behind the horses was a beautiful mountain range. This range of mountains was more beautiful than any on earth that I can remember seeing before.

Not fully understanding what I had just been shown, I rose up to leave. When, I turned around to walk away, I immediately noticed that the highway that was once behind me about a mile away, was gone. In its place was the range of mountains, which I had just seen in the vision.

My brother Dale wanted me to go with him to see his architect. He wanted me to see the architectural rendering of the home he was about to build. So, I agreed to accompany him, and we left. As we approached the office, which was an old beautifully converted house, we had to walk up a flight of stairs, as his architect was on the second story. Ascending the first flight of stairs, we came to a landing which would lead to his office. As we came to this landing I saw a sign which read: *Hardships are good as they develop stamina for the tough times ahead.* (Roman 5:3-5)

What does it all mean? The Lord told me that the multiplicity of horses represents every nation in the earth. The automobiles from the 60s represent the times we are going to be going back to in terms of modern conveniences. All the modern conveniences we have acquired since the 60s are going to be lost due to the immense hardships we are going to be experiencing. The fact that I saw the beautiful mountains in the vision, and then turned around and saw the same mountains behind me, means the following: The ocean will be claiming the land clear up to the mountains, behind will be a prairie type of land. Tough times ahead, but they are a means of strengthening us for even greater hardships. So, be thankful for your struggles today, that you may be prepared in God's grace for tomorrow.

I would also like to add here that this seizure of land by the ocean is minimal. For, in the very end times we will see much more of California gone due to earthquakes and a major tidal wave.

———— ✦ ————

5/97 A VISION

"HUMILITY"

I had a vision while waking this morning. The Lord said: *"It is humility to turn away from something you want very badly when it pleases the Lord for you to do so."*

———— ✦ ————

"FOR CANADA"

Again the word of the Lord came unto me saying, Son of man, set thy face against Zidon and prophesy against it. And say, Thus saith the Lord God: Behold I am against thee, O Zidon; and I will be glorified in the midst of thee: and they shall know that I am the Lord, when I shall have executed judgments in her, and shall be sanctified in her. For I will send into her pestilence, and blood into her streets; and the wounded shall be judged in the midst of her by sword upon her every side; and they shall know that I am the Lord. (Ezekiel 28:20-23)

I received this from the Lord when I was praising Him for the wonderful city in which, I was ministering in the province of Saskatchewan. He spoke to me very clearly saying: *"This city is not wonderful! Say not to Me: 'oh this city is wonderful;' for they have left me, for the lust of their own sin-sick flesh. They are given to every kind of evil, and daily practice witchcraft in this city, My children are not being taught my ways and the man of wickedness owns this city. I am not their God, for they love the gods of their own making, gods of silver and gold. Do not say to Me "Oh this wonderful city!" for this city is under My judgment. For I have given them My protection; and My blessings to this city have been great. But they have not given Me the honor or glory I am due for all I have done for them. They love their sorceries, their gambling and their greed, they do not love or reverence Me. Therefore, I shall be glorified in their midst through judgment. Yet, I have saved Me out a people to whom I will show myself strong. I will protect them and I will keep them in the hour of danger. So, tell My people to be holy, for I am holy. Tell My people to weep for Canada, for I Myself will weep for her in the day of her destruction."*

———— ✦ ————

5/97 A VISION

"EZEKIEL'S ARMY"

I saw what God is about to do in His Church. On May the 26th the Lord spoke to me about it very clearly. On the 27th I saw it in a vision. Again on June 14th I saw it in a vision. However, this time it was accompanied with deep travail and some instruction.

I saw a valley that was surrounded by a range of mountains that were far in the distance. However, this valley was more like a desert plain. Strewn from one end of the plain to the other lay the skeletal remains of human beings. They were not whole skeletons, but detached pieces of human skeletons. The wind was dry and arid and the time of day looked about dusk.

Then came the instruction from the Holy Spirit: "*Prophesy to these bones and say to them, Oh you dry bones hear the word of the Lord. Behold, I will cause breath and spirit to enter you, and you shall live. And, I will lay sinews upon you and bring up flesh upon you and cover you with skin, and I will put breath in you, and you dry bones shall live. Suddenly I saw the bones coming together, bone to bone, then I saw sinews upon the bones, and flesh came upon them.' The Spirit of the Lord then commanded me: 'Prophesy to the breath and spirit! Son of man and say to the breath and spirit, Thus says the Lord God: Come from the four winds, O breath and spirit, and breath upon these slain that they may live. So, I did as He told me, and breath and spirit entered into them and they lived and they stood upright, an army fit for war.* This is exactly what occurred as I travailed before the Lord. And that is exactly how it will happen in the Church. God is going to intervene. Those who cannot revive themselves, God will revive, so long as there is a heart to be revived. He will purge the sin that keeps the body slain, and He will give us life through His own holiness." (*Excerpt taken from the K.J.*)

"THE HOLOCAUST"

Recently, I was given a Messianic Jewish newspaper to read. After reading some of the heart-rending stories in it, I found myself weeping again for Israel. I rose up and went over to look out my window and looked up to the Father to pray. I said to Him: "Lord it must have hurt you very deeply to see these atrocities against your firstborn." Before I could finish my sentence, the Lord appeared to me weeping. Tears of anguish were flowing down His divine, grief stricken face. I was so shocked by His appearance and the pain that I saw in

His face, pain such as I only remember seeing a couple other times in Him that I turned away and wept the harder. I saw in His face it seemed, every tear that was cried, every scream of pain and anguish that was bellowed, every hope that was broken and desecrated. I saw every heart that lost faith, every desperate parent who searched, albeit unsuccessfully for their child in a prison camp and every terror filled face of a little child who died never seeing their parents again. Jesus remembers every one, every name. Not one will He ever forget, no more than you or I would if we had lost our child. He remembers, and it is He that said; Vengeance is mine, says the Lord! Although, He would rather have repentance, that He might show mercy; for Jesus loves the oppressor as much as the oppressed. However, if repentance does not follow, He will show vengeance without mercy for the atrocities that have been committed.

Don't ever let anyone tell you that Jesus does not hurt over the holocaust. As it simply isn't true. No man, woman or child knew pain in any of the near total holocaust of the Jews that Jesus did not bear right along with them. Our Lord's pain being many times greater, as He has born the pain of the millions of Jews who have died in this way throughout Jewish history.

* * * * * * * *

This is the last of the revelations and visitations that I feel could pertain to you or in some way minister to you my Dear Reader. What I have not included, I have withheld because it was too personal for me to share, or as I said earlier, the revelation or visitation was given for a specific member of the body and not for general reading. So, I trust you were able to glean from these writings, valuable truths to live by. The Lord wants to have a relationship with everyone in His Church like He has given to me. So if you will press in to Him through prayer, study of the Word, and maintain a life of obedience, making Him your all; thus, turning from everything that offends Him, you to can live in the supernatural as He is teaching me to do. You can also know Him in increasingly greater depths as I am learning to do. Seek Him with all your heart, and He will be found of you! Don't be stingy with the time you spend in prayer, and feast upon the Word as though it was your very life, as it is. In this way, Jesus can lead you in the paths of ever-increasing fullness of Himself.

One last thing, I am not sharing these with you with the anticipation that you might consider them as you would Scripture. Encouragement, insight and instructions such as these are meant by the Holy Spirit to help you gain greater insight in His Word, not to replace it. So, remember to eat your meals out of His Word daily.

God bless you in your seeking, and Amen!

In His Amazing Love,

Nita Johnson

Nita Johnson

Name _____

Address _____

City/State/Zip _____

Phone (_____)_____ Today's Date _____

All Materials Are FREE of Charge.
Purchaser is Liable for Postage & Handling.
Canadian Customers Please Make Checks Payable To: NITA JOHNSON

NO.	TITLE
S100	GIFTS OF FIRE
S101	KEYS OF FAITH
S102	THE KINGDOM
S103	CHRIST AND THE BRIDE
S104	THE LIBERTY OF GRACE
S105	PRAYER POWER
S106	MELCHISEDEC
S107	PROPHETIC INSIGHT II
S108	PROPHETIC INSIGHT III
S109	PROPHETIC INSIGHT IV
S110	PROPHETIC INSIGHT V
S111	INTERCESSION
S112	THE WONDERS OF PRAYER
S113	UNITY
S114	LOVE REVIVAL
S115	VICTORY OVER THE CURSE
S116	PROBLEM OR OPPORTUNITY
S117	AGLOW WITH THE SPIRIT
S118	REVELATION THROUGH MEDITATION
S119	HOLINESS UNTO THE LORD
S120	SECRETS OF PRAYER
S121	PROPHECY CONFERENCE
S122	PROPHETIC INTERCESSORS CONFERENCE
100	PETER
101	FOR SINGLES ONLY
102	SPIRIT OF GIVING
BOOK	PREPARE FOR THE WINDS OF CHANGE II
BOOK	THE EVER SPEAKING VOICE OF GOD
BOOK	PUTTING ON THE BREASTPLATE OF RIGHTEOUSNESS

POSTAGE & HANDLING (call office for costs) $ _____

Future Publications soon to be released:
- CANTICLES OF THE EXCHANGED LIFE.
- WINNING THE VISION.
- THE OVERCOMING LIFE THROUGH PRAYER

THE WORLD FOR JESUS MINISTRIES, INC.
New Address Effective as of September 1998.
MSC #402
497 - N. Clovis Ave. #202
Clovis, CA 93611-0373

If you would like to receive our bi-monthly newsletter entitled: Prophetic Insight and Family Focus, free of charge please let us know.

It is a prophetic bulletin geared toward the family and will help you prepare for the days ahead.

We can be reached at:
Office (402) 498-3496
FAX   (402) 331-5175
or

EAGLES NEST PUBLISHING
A DIVISION OF WORLD FOR JESUS MINISTRIES

643 North 98th Street • Suite 146
Omaha, NE 68114-2332

New Address Effective as of September 1998.
MSC #402
497 - N. Clovis Ave. #202
Clovis, CA 93611-0373